W9-CDX-355

ISSUES THAT CONCERN YOU

Consumer Culture

Heidi Watkins, *Book Editor*

GREENHAVEN PRESS

A part of Gale, Cengage Learning

GALE
CENGAGE Learning

Detroit • New York • San Francisco • New Haven, Conn • Waterville, Maine • London

Christine Nasso, *Publisher*
Elizabeth Des Chenes, *Managing Editor*

© 2011 Greenhaven Press, a part of Gale, Cengage Learning

Gale and Greenhaven Press are registered trademarks used herein under license.

For more information, contact:
Greenhaven Press
27500 Drake Rd.
Farmington Hills, MI 48331-3535
Or you can visit our Internet site at gale.cengage.com

For product information and technology assistance, contact us at

Gale Customer Support, 1-800-877-4253
For permission to use material from this text or product, submit all requests online at
www.cengage.com/permissions

Further permissions questions can be e-mailed to permissionrequest@cengage.com

Articles in Greenhaven Press anthologies are often edited for length to meet page requirements. In addition, original titles of these works are changed to clearly present the main thesis and to explicitly indicate the author's opinion. Every effort is made to ensure that Greenhaven Press accurately reflects the original intent of the authors. Every effort has been made to trace the owners of copyrighted material.

Cover image copyright © Yuri Arcus / Shutterstock.com

LIBRARY OF CONGRESS CATALOGING-IN-PUBLICATION DATA

Consumer culture / Heidi Watkins, book editor.
   p. cm. -- (Issues that concern you)
  Includes bibliographical references and index.
  ISBN 978-0-7377-5206-9 (hardcover)
  1. Consumption (Economics)--Social aspects--United States. 2. Consumers--United States. 3. Materialism--Social aspects. I. Watkins, Heidi.
  HC110.C6C5622 2011
  306.30973--dc22

                                                2010038105

Printed in the United States of America
1 2 3 4 5 6 7 15 14 13 12 11

CONTENTS

Appendix

Imagine no grocery bills, completely free furniture, and free appliances—television, microwave, refrigerator—everything. How does Josh Corlew, a twenty-six-year-old who manages a nonprofit organization, do it? He does not steal things, nor does he still live with his parents or mooch off his friends. Corlew is a "freegan," a term derived from *free* and *vegan*. He prefers the term "consumer conscious," but the ideals and lifestyle are the same: abandoning a consumer-driven lifestyle for the joys of dumpster diving.

Not all freegans are the same. Some, like Corlew, make a decent living and work regular, full-time jobs; others turn to freeganism out of necessity—to get by on limited means (interestingly, some of these freegans stick with it long after they do not need to, financially); some, feeling empty, leave prestigious and lucrative careers to join the freegan community. There are different degrees of freeganism as well. Some freegans hold full- or part-time jobs, drive cars, and own homes; others, who might be considered "true freegans," are more radical, viewing freeganism as an entire lifestyle and a full-time pursuit. Refusing to purchase anything, they use bicycles as their only transportation, squat in abandoned houses, live in small trailers or urban encampments, and barter for whatever they do not find for free.

Freegans share the same motivations, however: to lessen their participation in and to protest a wasteful consumer society. According to Corlew, "'bin diving' or 'dumpstering' is as much a war on wretched excess as anything else. This is about distancing myself from the consumerism of America. . . . Every time we buy something, we're saying we support the system that brought it about."[1]

Another freegan, Michael J. Foster, explains it this way: "New York City is a land of waste. In 2002, according to the city's Department of Sanitation, New York generated 832,590 tons of food waste. Freegans have figured out a way to recover these lost calories, and by doing so we have made our actions in protest and education . . . because we scavenge visibly and without embarrassment, we demonstrate to others that they can choose to opt out of capitalism . . . that consumerism is a choice."[2]

Additionally, freegans may find a personal sense of liberation or freedom by rejecting consumerism. According to Ryan Beiler, a dumpster diver in the Washington, D.C., area, "Dumpstering's spontaneity is both liberating and satisfying. Instead of the anxiety of bargain-hunting among the throngs at the übermarkets, I enjoy the surprises of late-night expeditions and never worry about finding enough to eat." Beiler also considers never worrying about what he will eat a spiritual aspect of freeganism that has strengthened his faith, describing freeganism as "a subversive option for living a frugal yet abundant life."[3]

Indeed, freegans are not talking about moldy fruit, day-old donuts, or sour milk. An evening's catch might be something like:

- "ten tubs of yogurt, sell-by date tomorrow; broccoli with one sad spear and four richly green stalks; a five-pound sack of turnips; a case of somewhat brown but delicious bananas; five bags of Oreos . . . hundreds of bagels, unspoiled with used coffee grounds, so fresh that the bag was still warm."[4]
- "trash bags full of bagels so fresh that when they were opened, the air filled with the aroma of freshly baked bread . . . canned goods and even toilet paper."[5]
- "parsnips, bay leaves, and sorrel for your dinner [found] in Brooklyn's Prospect Park."[6]

Some freegans even find themselves eating better than they normally would. Beiler describes finding at different times pounds of smoked salmon and several jars of caviar and regularly enjoys grocery store sushi (nothing with raw meat) and gourmet bread.

While freegans may wax euphoric and sound like they are describing a hidden utopia for the taking, freeganism has its critics who point to the dangers of dumpster diving. Besides putting oneself at risk by lurking around and crawling in dumpsters in dark places at night, dumpster diving is illegal in many cities and states

Freegans are people who have abandoned the consumer-driven lifestyle in favor of dumpster diving.

and even if not, may be considered trespassing. Enforcement of bans on dumpster diving also varies by city and state, however.

The first risk that probably comes to mind, however, is the possible contaminants in the discarded food that freegans will eventually put into their mouths. Critics argue that even if the food itself is safe, bacteria may be present in the trash containers and contaminate it. In fact, one in thirty dumpster divers reported illness from dumpster foods in a study published in the journal *Australian Geographer*. The sample size in this study was only thirty however, and the illness was most likely caused by shrink-wrapped mushrooms found in a hot climate, a dumpster find that could and should have been avoided.

Freegans themselves argue that common sense must prevail. They avoid dairy, raw meat, anything that smells bad, looks moldy, or seems to be near something contaminated. Furthermore, they will point out that grocery store meat is probably more of a risk than dumpster vegetables. Steve Kolowich, a Princeton University student who studies and practices freeganism, says, "I've never gotten sick from Dumpster-diving, and I've never talked to anyone who has gotten sick from it. . . . The freegan's claim is that there's more bacteria in the meat that you get from the supermarket than from a vegan item you get from the trash." Furthermore, most of what freegans use is packaged food or in plastic bags, according to Alf Montague, who says, "Essentially it is quality wealth that is being discarded."[7]

Critics of freeganism also point to freegans' ideals, saying that freegans are not so altruistic because they are living off of capitalism and consumer waste and therefore are depending on or even contributing to the system. Freegans are quick to defend themselves, however. According to Montague, "It's been argued that freegans actually live off capitalism. . . . But it's about waste. There are enough resources in the world to share with everyone. People shared long before capitalism. It's all about learning to live off less, appreciate what you have and sharing what you don't need. People have been encouraged through capitalism to fight each other for the world's resources."[8]

Freeganism is a hard sell for most people. If nothing else, it causes most people to pause and think about consumer consumption. Furthermore, freeganism is not the only possible answer to overconsumption. Many people find it more practical just to buy less, waste less, buy used items, and share what they do have.

Consumer culture is a complicated issue and a matter worthy of discussion for professionals as well as today's students. The articles in this volume represent multiple viewpoints surrounding the issue. It is hoped that they will help you understand the issue more fully, yet also see it in its full complexity.

Notes

1. Quoted in Michelle Conlin, "In the Land of Plenty, Why Pay?" *BusinessWeek*, October 20, 2008.

2. Michael J. Foster, "1,000 Bagels a Night or: How I Learned to Stop Worrying and Love NYC Garbage," *Earth Island Journal*, Spring 2008, p. 64.

3. Ryan Beiler, "The Tao of Dumpster Diving. Why Scavenge? You Get a Lot of Really Good Food That's Really, Really Free," *Sojourner's*, May 2006.

4. Foster, "1,000 Bagels a Night or: How I learned to Stop Worrying and Love NYC Garbage."

5. Raina Kelley, "Are Freegans Oddballs or Sages? *Newsweek*'s Raina Kelley Spent a Month Living as One to Find Out," *Newsweek*, October 1, 2007, p. 46.

6. Kelley, "Are Freegans Oddballs or Sages?"

7. Quoted in Sergio Burns, "A Freegan World," *In These Times*, September 7, 2007.

8. Quoted in Burns, "A Freegan World."

ONE

Consumer Culture Harms Society

Benjamin Barber, interview by Kimberly Palmer

> In this e-mail interview with *U.S. News & World Report*, Benjamin Barber, a political writer and author of *Consumed: How Markets Corrupt Children, Infantilize Adults, and Swallow Citizens Whole*, explains his ideas about consumer culture to Kimberly Palmer, a financial writer for *U.S. News*. Barber maintains that short-term gratification, a focus on shopping, and pop culture have replaced America's work ethic and left its citizens with little time for activities that nurture humans, such as art, friendship, spirituality, and thinking.

In *Consumed: How Markets Corrupt Children, Infantilize Adults, and Swallow Citizens Whole*, political theorist and University of Maryland Prof. Benjamin Barber argues that we have shifted from a "work hard" ethic to one that idealizes immediate gratification and selfishness. In the process, he says, we have lost our sense of civic responsibility. He points to high divorce rates, adults who act the way kids do, and the glorification of shopping as Americans' new national pastime. In an E-mail interview, *U.S. News* asked him why he was so dismayed with consumer culture.

What is wrong with a culture that glorifies consumerism?

A culture that glorifies consumerism belittles other values, including all those activities that define nonmaterial life and give us our human character: play, prayer, art, love, recreation, creativity, friendship, and thought. The problem with consumerism is that it strives not just to be part of our lives—it should be that—but strives to be everything, to occupy all our time and space and push out other things. In this sense, it is both homogenizing and totalizing.

If short-term gratification is replacing hard work, as you say, will our productivity and economic growth decrease over time?

At present, we manage to both work too hard and work too hard at playing. We are productive materially but increasingly unproductive creatively, ethically, spiritually, and in other ways. We focus hard on the now—work and play—but forget how to invest in the future and defer gratification to increase real satisfaction. In this way, we move away from the "Protestant ethos" of early "productivist capitalism" and fall into the lassitude of late "consumerist capitalism." We work like hell but work in order to play and play by consuming.

You criticize aspects of pop culture, such as Hollywood movies, for turning adults into children. But isn't it just allowing them to buy the kind of entertainment they most want? In other words, maybe adults are really just kids at heart, and pop culture allows them to be themselves.

Those who shape and condition our "wants and needs" by manufacturing needs to sell all the goods they produce do what those with influence and power have always done: claim that they are merely giving people "what they want." Yet aside from the fact they spend billions of dollars a year in advertising and marketing to "help" people "want" what they are producing, they also leave little room for the kinds of alternative nonchildish goods we might actually want, if given half a chance.

Limited multiplex movie screens rarely show "serious" films, and despite the supposed variety of television, there is a commercial sameness to much of what is shown. So I would say not that pop culture "lets people be themselves" but rather [that it]

In response to bargain-day sales, consumers, in their shopping fervor, often act like small children unrestrained at a candy store.

creates a flat and homogenous kind of self that it then encourages them to "become"—or pretends they already are.

What kidlike behaviors do you engage in?

I make a distinction between childlike or kidlike behavior that is spontaneous, playful, and creative and doesn't cost money to engage in, and the kinds of infantilized behaviors that demand shopping and consuming as a condition for being mindless and impetuous. I myself (like all of us, I suspect) enjoy being childlike at times: playing with my kids and grandkids, indulging in games, enjoying silliness.

But I don't think that buying things and having 2-year-olds watching Baby Einstein or Baby First TV has very much to do with real childhood. The irony is that even as it dumbs down adults to turn them into shopaholic consumers, the market tries to get kids to grow up quick into little consumers who spend all their parents' discretionary income!

You talk about the fact that the marketplace makes people think they "need" things that they really don't. Do you find yourself falling victim to this?

Yes, I think we all tend to buy into fads and "push marketing" consumables that we are convinced we can't get along without. You know, the latest Michael Jordan high-top or that oh-so-cool iPhone or that bottle of tap water in the gorgeous bottle. I recently almost bought a luxury hybrid, kidding myself that I could somehow have a power car and help Al Gore save the environment. Until someone pointed out that it got worse mileage than the same nonhybrid model! Marketing works! Even on "educated consumers." That's why companies spend billions on it. That's why it's so pernicious.

What's your advice to people who want to resist being "consumed" by the modern marketplace?

Talk to family and friends about what your real needs are. . . . Do you have to have that latest gadget, or might real happiness come from spending some time with them (for free!) walking or talking? Ask yourself whether you would really "want" to buy something if you hadn't read that cool ad or seen your rival with it.

Think not about what you "want" but what you think would be good for your kids, your neighborhood, and your community. Often when we change the subject from "me" to "we," many artificial wants and needs melt away and the really important things come into focus. Think as a citizen as well as consumer.

You describe consumerism as pretty severe. Could it get any worse in the coming decades?

The bad can always get worse. As capitalism fulfills our real needs and wants, it tends to manufacture phony and faux [false] needs to keep selling us stuff. But there are countertrends. Capitalism can also revert to meeting real needs, of which there are plenty in the modern world. Instead of selling us $20 billion a year in bottled water, we can get clean and free from the tap, it can help solve the world water shortage and help get billions of people without clean water access.

There are signs that young people are looking for alternative music, alternative art, and alternative lifestyles that don't just depend on consuming stuff. So while consumerism is all-consuming, there is hope—if we are willing to take the problem seriously and act like grown-ups.

You write, "The family hearth is no longer a refuge in a world of virtual commerce where the tentacles of the digital octopus stretch out around the family gatekeepers and into the child's bedroom and

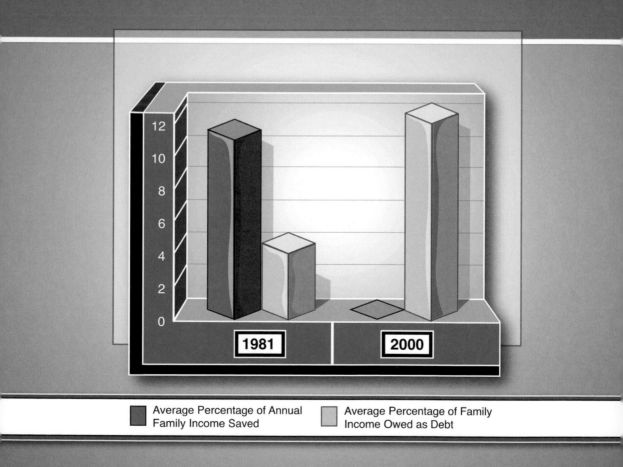

Trends in Consumer Saving vs. Spending

- Average Percentage of Annual Family Income Saved
- Average Percentage of Family Income Owed as Debt

Taken from: *Christian Science Monitor,* "Why Can't Americans Save a Dime?" *MSN Money Central.*
http://moneycentral.msn.com/content/savinganddebt/savemoney/p145775.asp.

computer and television screens." Even though our televisions and Internet connections blare advertisements and focus on short-term gratification, is it possible, at some point, to turn those off and experience rich inner lives?

Of course it is. Humans like material things but love what goes beyond the material. We want consumables but need human comfort, religious experience, civic commonality, creative expression, and many other activities that cannot be bought. We may be addicted to shopping, but we long for comfort—which can be found only in knowledge or art or family or religion or love. So yes, turn off the TV, go offline, and try living with the gifts we are born with. The things we can't put a price on are the things we most prize. Just try it.

TWO

Consumer Culture Benefits Society

Howard Bloom

> Howard Bloom, a science writer and former music indus-
> try publicist, is the author of *The Genius of the Beast:
> A Radical Re-Vision of Capitalism*. Here, in an article for
> Scientific Blogging, he challenges readers to examine the
> assumption that consumer culture is bad for individuals
> and society. He examines the life of nineteenth-century
> philosopher Henry David Thoreau, author of *Walden*,
> a book that advocates living simply in nature. While
> acknowledging the positive contributions of Thoreau's
> ideas, Bloom argues that the industrial era and consum-
> erism of Thoreau's day not only made Thoreau's writing
> possible but improved the lives of individuals and society
> as a whole.

There's a rule of science we normally overlook. That rule?
Challenge your assumptions. See what you can derive from
a new point of view. Buck the normal. Today, it is normal to
hate consumerism. It's normal to loathe what consumerism has
done to us . . . and what it has done to the planet. So as good
scientists, let's go anti-conventional. Let's sing an ode in praise
of consumerism. Let's see if reversing the normal point of view
will produce any surprises.

Howard Bloom, "In Praise of Consumerism—It Appeals to the Thoreau in You," *Scientific
Blogging*, April 18, 2008. Reproduced by permission.

In praise of consumerism? I know what you're thinking; this is a great subject for the brain-dead or folks who utterly lack a moral compass, like Donald Trump and Paris Hilton. But it's certainly not a good subject for you and me.

You're not consumerists, and neither am I, right? We're idealists aiming at high spiritual and intellectual goals. We scrimp and we save to gain the freedom to think and to pursue higher meanings in nearly everything we do.

Or are we?

You and I didn't call the toll-free 800 number on our TV screen and lay out $600 for Sharper Image's Ionic Breeze air purifier. We didn't whip out our cellphones when the boob tube tempted us to commit to a lifetime of easy $20 payments for the Bowflex exercise machine, no matter how scrumptious that infomercial's hyper-tanned and hyper-toned 50-year-old grandmother was in her black bikini.

I don't know about you, but I even passed on $19.95 for the instant-heating soldering iron you can carry in your pocket to your grandmother's house, then use on the spot to rewire the place.

Who Owns Whom?

During the last hundred and fifty years, ever since Henry David Thoreau's *Walden* and Karl Marx's *Communist Manifesto*, two books written at pretty much the same time, the question brought up by my material possessions and by yours has been this: who exactly owns whom? Do I own my things or do my things own me?

The answer has traditionally been that my things, and the folks who made them, are manipulating me like puppetmasters. In the old days, as recently as before you started reading this article, the goal would have been to send you out with your heads drooping in shame, convinced that we've got to toss out all of our stuff and escape the tyranny of things.

But yesterday's cliche should always be up for review. And today we're going to review it heavily. Why? Because, for one thing, doing what I do for thrills and delight, trying to open minds and uplift spirits, is a strange business. The spirit and the mind depend on massive heaps of exactly what we're supposed to loathe and toss away—material possessions, consumer goods, and gadgets marketed by multinational companies. Feeding curiosity and opening new insights takes credit cards and cash.

A False Separation

Does this mean that the dichotomy between materialism and spiritualism are false? Does it mean that the body and the spirit are not boxers in opposite corners of the ring? Does it mean that we climb toward the heavens of intellect and of enlightenment on a ladder of material possessions? Yes, I'm afraid it does. The long and short of it is this: The human spirit dances on higher and higher stages every generation. And each of those stages is held aloft by material things.

If I'm so right about materialism, why have so many generations of philosophers far brighter than I am gotten it wrong? Why did Socrates, Plato, Marcus Aurelius, Spinoza, and Mahatma Gandhi insist on a Spartan way of life?

To answer the question, let's get specific and put just one great thinker under the microscope—Henry David Thoreau, author of *Walden Pond* and of *On Civil Disobedience*. In roughly 1842, why was Thoreau so easily able to insist on chucking the material way of life, going off to Walden Pond, and living in utter simplicity for roughly two years? Why was he able to toss aside technology and wealth so he could see more in a walk around Concord than the rich kids of his day saw on their steamship trips to Europe? Why was he able to say, "A man is rich in proportion to the number of things which he can afford to let alone."

A Cathedral and a Leaf

Here are a few of the answers:

Answer number one: *Thoreau had the gift of wonder*. He could see more in a leaf than most men and women can see in a cathedral. But guess what a cathedral and a leaf have in common? They're both material things. And guess what else they have in common?

They're both consumer goods. One is an item we humans use to show off. It's a status symbol. That's the cathedral. The other is the ultimate throwaway and pawn in a plant's competitive game. It's nature's version of litter, the disposable solar panel, the leaf.

There's another thing the leaf and the cathedral have in common: They're both material platforms from which the spirit can draw epiphanies [revelations]. Providing platforms for epiphany is precisely what the material realm is all about, at least it is if you keep your eyes wide open. If you look with wonder and ingenuity. And if you don't have epiphanies, Evolution surely will.

More on that in the next installment. First, back to Thoreau and to our question: Why was Henry David Thoreau able to chuck the material way of life, go off to Walden Pond, and live in utter simplicity, shedding technology and wealth so he could see more in a walk around Concord than the rich kids of his day saw on their steamship trips to Europe?

A New Utopia

Here comes answer number two. *Henry David Thoreau was a rich kid.* And not just any old rich kid. He was the ultimate beneficiary of the Industrial Revolution. Thoreau's dad owned a pencil factory. Which meant that Thoreau's privileged position came from a boom of literacy, a boom in the use of writing tools, a boom in the growth of offices, and a boom in the new way of making things, a boom in mass production.

Alexander Hamilton wrote a prophetic position paper approximately fifty years before Thoreau abandoned everything and lived with nature. In 1792 Hamilton wrote "A Report On The Subject Of Manufactures," a radically futuristic essay about a whole new kind of utopia.

Hamilton's words glowed as he wrote breathlessly about a new way of organizing machinery and human energy, a new system invented in England that would set American farm women and farm children free from the gloom, the boredom, and the hunger that winter forced upon them. This new machine-plus-human combo would make old forms of drudgery so easy-on-the-muscles

Alexander Hamilton prophetically wrote in his "A Report On The Subject Of Manufactures" about new ways of organizing machinery and human energy to set people free from daily drudgery.

that women and kids could make money during the dreariest months of the year.

The new system would free even children to earn spare change. How? By tending to the levers and cogs in the workplaces of Hamilton's brave new future—in the next-tech churches of inexpensive goods and of mass production—factories. Alexander Hamilton's vision was on the money. It was so smack on target that fifty years after Hamilton penned his prophecies, the profits of a pencil-making factory gave Henry David Thoreau the leisure time for philosophy.

Another 50 years after Walden Pond, we'd reinterpret Alexander Hamilton's utopia—and the source of Thoreau's freedom. Hamilton had foreseen the liberation of farm kids from a winter of hunger, cold, and poverty, liberation into jobs that would keep them warm, feed their families, and fill their pockets with spending money. We now call that new freedom "child labor." So Thoreau was free to write "Go confidentally in the direction of your dreams! Live the life you've imagined. As you simplify your life, the laws of the universe will be simpler." Wonderful words and I believe in most of them. But they were the fruits of child labor.

Escape from Technology?

Here's answer number three to the question of why Thoreau could chuck material goods and technology and go with mother nature, at least for a few winters: *Thoreau never chucked technology at all. He pretended it didn't exist.* The winter in which Thoreau made most of his notes for Walden Pond was icy as could be. It was so icy that industrial workers showed up regularly to saw the three-foot-thick crust of ice from Walden Pond's surface and take it to insulated warehouses where it could be kept frozen and sold in summer to refrigerate the food of rich folks from the city.

In that winter freeze, did Thoreau really escape technology? You be the judge. Mother nature didn't build the cabin in which Thoreau lived. 125,000 generations of human ingenuity made the axes, saws, and mills that allowed men to fell trees and to slice their trunks into boards inexpensively. A thousand generations of even more techno-lust and techno-innovation went into inventing the wall, the floor, the roof, and the frame of beams and joists that holds a cabin upright.

Clothes as Technology

Mother Nature didn't weave the clothes that Thoreau wore to keep from freezing to death. In fact, by 1842, when Thoreau went off to commune with nature, the cotton he wore was raised on what we'd call industrial agricultural farms—plantations. That cotton carried the ingenuity of 500 generations of farmers and of genetic tinkerers who had turned a wild plant that made fuzz to carry its seeds into a tame plant, one genetically tweaked to concentrate its energies on churning out the fiber that was valued by human beings.

Thoreau's clothes were made by mechanical looms invented just 90 years before he went off to ponder by the pond side. Those mechanical looms were powered either by water-driven mills or by steam engines; power hook-ups developed just seventeen years before Thoreeau was born.

Thoreau's clothes were laundered using soap whose chemical manufacture had been worked out by two French chemists. In 1791 Nicholas Leblanc patented a process for making soda ash—one key soap ingredient—from mere salt. Twenty years later, Michel Eugene Chevreul figured out the answer to a mystery; exactly what kind of fats make soap. That insight led to soap's mass manufacture. Then came the first and maybe greatest consumer marketing blitz in history.

Folks had lived for 35,000 years in clothes they seldom changed. Why? Clothes were so expensive that in Arabia, desert tribes raided and killed each other just to get a few armfuls of other people's robes. The clothes of the pre–Industrial Age were based on animal fiber—wool and felt. They housed thousands of insects that lived off your skin and blood, sapping your energy every day. And you didn't want to bathe. Getting wet could mean that the merest draft could give you a cold. And a cold in those good old days often led to something worse, pneumonia, an illness that could kill you.

Soap as Technology

Once the new machinery of Thoreau's day made plant-based clothing, cotton clothing, cheap, the new soap industry put on one of the first major advertising and marketing blitzes. That blitz laid the foundation for what we now call consumerism—selling us mass-produced goods by using another human invention, mass media.

That pioneering advertising tide produced a perception-shift in the Western mind. It convinced the West that new forms of personal hygiene were not just desirable but mandatory. It convinced the average European and American that, "You can measure a civilization by the number of times it washes a day.". . .

The Soap and Cotton Revolution gave Henry David Thoreau the luxury of spending his winter by Walden Pond without fearing for his health at every turn. It did something even more important for the readers Thoreau was writing for. It extended the average human lifespan by 20 years!!!

Meanwhile a boom of affordable housing gave Thoreau the elbow-room to say, "Our houses are such unwieldy property that we are often imprisoned rather than housed in them." To make a statement like that you have to take the conquest of one of humankind's toughest challenges for granted; the need for a roof (or at least a cave) over your head.

And here's another thing to ponder. What's the relationship between the new Industrial Revolution's flood of ready-made shirts, pants, jackets, and cravats and the casual assumptions that allowed Thoreau to say, "It is an interesting question how far men would retain their relative rank if they were divested of their clothes."

Books as Technology

But, again, back to Thoreau's attempt to escape the complications of technology. Here's a blunt fact to ponder. Thoreau was writing his notes with a published book in mind. When he penned his famous phrase, "The mass of men lead lives of quiet desperation," he took it for granted that some of those desperate men would spend their days in printing plants tending the machines that mass-produced the ultimate elevators of the spirit, a consumer item called books.

Add to all of that a fact that frequently slips out of our sight. Thoreau's sojourn at Walden Pond was the product of the ultimate Industrial Era luxury—spare time. Not that there hadn't

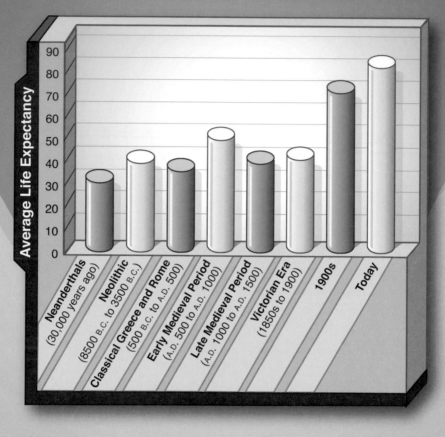

Changes in Average Life Expectancy

Average Life Expectancy

- Neanderthals (30,000 years ago)
- Neolithic (8500 B.C. to 3500 B.C.)
- Classical Greece and Rome (500 B.C. to A.D. 500)
- Early Medieval Period (A.D. 500 to A.D. 1000)
- Late Medieval Period (A.D. 1000 to A.D. 1500)
- Victorian Era (1850s to 1900s)
- 1900s
- Today

Taken from: Judy Steed, "It's Never Too Late to Grow Your Brain," *Toronto Star*, November 13, 2008.

been idle moments in the past, there had been. But they'd been reserved for a thin crust of landed aristocrats, not for the middle class, not for the sons of entrepreneurs, not for the sons of tradesmen, and not for the sons of manufacturers like Thoreau.

Thoreau as a Consumer

Only a man who is certain he'll have food, clothing, and shelter every day can say, "The finest qualities of our nature, like the bloom on fruits, can be preserved only by the most delicate handling. Yet we do not treat ourselves nor one another thus tenderly."

So Henry David Thoreau wrote meditations on the human spirit, on nature, on Civil Disobedience—a term he coined—and on new, mass-produced, mass-media-dependent forms of protest against government injustices. He said nasty things about Industrial mankind, things like "Thank God men cannot as yet fly and lay waste the sky as well as the earth!"

In other words, he wrote some of the key documents in the evolution of the anti-consumerist, pro-nature sentiments we see today. With his books, he lifted my spirits high when I was sixteen years old and gave me new conceptual tools with which to crusade for meaning, meaning for my world and for yours.

He gave me a part of my sense of mission. He probably did the same for you, which means that Henry David Thoreau's spiritual contributions were enormous. But they were all based on new material goods, new forms of producing them, and new ways of marketing them.

Henry David Thoreau's meditations on the human spirit were built on a solid base of material overflow, they were built on a base of consumerism.

THREE

Consumer Culture Harms Children and Teens

Madeline Levine

A practicing clinical psychologist for more than twenty-five years, Madeline Levine, author of the book *The Price of Privilege*, has witnessed firsthand the effects of consumer culture on teens. Here, in an essay for *Tikkun* magazine, a bimonthly publication of the Network of Spiritual Progressives, she explains the crises of privileged youth, citing that depression among girls from affluent families is three times the national norm and providing examples of teens in consumer-driven families who, despite their monetary advantages, struggle with emptiness. She analyzes the negative effects of materialism on families and provides alternatives to consumer culture that will build stronger children.

Our country has a new group of "at-risk" kids. They don't belong to the group traditionally considered "at-risk"—inner city kids growing up in harsh economic circumstances. Surprisingly, they belong to the upper middle class, to parents who have comfortable incomes and high levels of education. Current research tells us that it is children of privilege, children long assumed to be protected from elevated rates of emotional problems that are, in fact, evidencing the *highest* rates of emotional problems of any group of kids in this country.

These numbers remind us that there are myths at both ends of the socio-economic spectrum. Many of us assume that the economic and social challenges of poverty are so severe that parenting skills and child development are compromised. Alternately, many assume that in families where parents are financially secure and highly educated, both parenting skills and child development are enhanced. Research tells us that neither assumption is correct. In fact, pre-teens and teens from affluent homes have the highest rates of depression, anxiety disorders and substance abuse of any group of children in this country.

There is something unsettling and paradoxical about this fact. After all, these same youngsters are the recipients of both high levels of parental involvement as well as extensive educational, extra-curricular, and recreational opportunities. Is it possible that some combination of money, opportunity, and involvement is having a toxic rather than a protective effect on kids? And if so, what can parents do to make sure that being privileged works toward healthy emotional development rather than against it?

Troubled Kids

Adolescence has long been thought of as a period of heightened confusion and unhappiness. In fact, adolescents are no more likely to be clinically depressed (as opposed to normally conflicted) than any other age group. So when researchers find that 22 percent of girls from affluent families are clinically depressed—that's three times the national rate—and that somewhere between 30 and 40 percent of teens from privileged backgrounds have significant psychological symptoms, we have, according to the definition used by the CDC (Centers for Disease Control) in Atlanta, reached an "epidemic."

This epidemic should disturb all of us, no matter our background. Kids from affluent homes, *because* of the educational and financial opportunities available to them often grow into positions of leadership and authority. Our future doctors, lawyers,

CEOs, and policy makers need to be emotionally robust and to have [a] well-defined sense of right and wrong. Mental health problems compromise good decision making.

Ironically, I began to realize the depth of this epidemic—and to write the book that became *The Price of Privilege*—when I met a girl who was particularly adept at hiding her illness from friends and family. Allison was a seemingly typical new patient in my practice made up largely of the daughters and occasionally the sons of well-to-do parents in Marin County, California. She was a well groomed and polite fifteen-year-old who walked into my office with the kind of confidence I often see among my young patients. But Allison's distress was easy for me to read. She was wearing the kind of T-shirt that those in the business of adolescent mental health instantly recognize as a "cutter's T-shirt," a shirt with the cuff pulled low to hide the wrist and a hole for the thumb. These T-shirts are often worn by young girls trying to camouflage the cutting that they do on their wrists and forearms.

When I commented on Allison's T-shirt, she willingly showed me what she had done to herself only hours earlier—taken a razor and incised the word "EMPTY" into her forearm. Allison's "EMPTY" helped crystallize my thoughts about what exactly I had been seeing in my office for the past several years—kids who for all the world looked fine on the outside, but were bleeding underneath. Kids who looked like they had everything, but in fact had none of the things that are necessary to anchor a healthy sense of self: a sense of authenticity, of purpose, of being loved for who they are and not simply how they perform. For Allison, as for many of my young patients, the development of a sense of self was stalled.

Perplexed Parents

Allison's parents, like most of the parents in my practice, are involved, concerned, loving, and very demanding. They tend to motivate Allison with material goods like expensive pocketbooks and designer jeans. They are very proud of their child's academic and athletic accomplishments, but seem to have little understanding

Depression, Anxiety, and Alcohol Use Among Girls from Wealthy Families

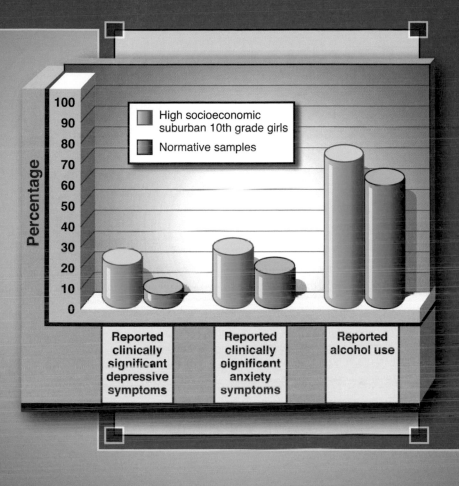

Taken from: Suniya S. Luthar and Bronwyn E. Becker, "Privileged but Pressured? A Study of Affluent Youth," *Child Development*, September/October 2002.

of Allison's distress. They are more than a bit angry that after all they've done, their daughter appears ungrateful. However, they are also terribly worried about Allison's cutting and escalating depression, and are hoping that with some therapy and "a little medication," she'll get back to her old self. In fact, Allison does need help—help understanding why she has given up on herself, why she feels so empty, and why she is so reliant on external praise and recognition to feel good about herself.

Yet to help Allison, as in so many of these cases, her parents also must be helped. These privileged parents need to learn some of the basic tenets of child development: that a sense of self is crafted from the inside out; that parental love cannot be conditional on performance; and that emotional availability—not simply car-time racing from one activity to the next—is what helps kids develop a robust sense of self as well as a reliable repertoire of coping skills that help them to navigate through the inevitable challenges of life.

Unfortunately, good intentions are not the same as good parenting skills. Parents today focus too much on what they can do for their children and on what they can give to their children, instead of concentrating on being available for their children. In the words of one of my astute patients: "It's amazing that my mother can be everywhere and nowhere at the same time." The levels of anxiety we have about whether our child will get into the right preschool, the right elementary school, the right high school, and ultimately the right college, used to be reserved for issues of life and death.

Whether our child gets into this school or that simply is not that important. Research has consistently shown that the college one attends has *no* relationship to how happy one will be in life, nor for that matter does it correlate with how much money one will make. Our tremendous preoccupation with grabbing the brass ring, competing with those around us, and winning at all costs, has sent a clear message to our children—that what matters most in life is competition, individualism and the things we accumulate. Instead, we should be teaching our children the values of cooperation, reciprocity and connection. We need to turn our attention from the surfaces of life and let our children know that what we really value is the substance—how we value ourselves, how we treat others, and our ability to walk in someone else's shoes.

Children learn by watching and imitating their parents. This should not be news to anyone. Before we can teach our children good values, we have to gut check our own values.

The Problem Is Not Money—It's Materialism

Acknowledging that children of privilege are experiencing unacceptably high rates of emotional distress is a good beginning, but it doesn't address the cause of these problems. It is not money per se that stalls emotional development. Rather, researchers have found a number of variables that appear to be driving the high rates of depression, anxiety disorders and substance abuse among upper-middle-class kids.

1. *Kids are excessively pressured.* Voltaire said, "The enemy of the good is better." When kids sit weeping in my office because they received a B instead of an A on an exam, or when a child is too afraid to go home, anticipating his father's disappointment when he finds his son has been cut from the varsity team, we have made it clear that our kids are only as good as their last performance. This makes for anxious kids who can't attend to the normal challenges of growing up because they are so worried about maintaining parental approval, often at all costs.

2. *Kids feel disconnected from their parents.* Research shows that upper-middle-class kids feel more disconnected from their parents than children from any other socio-economic group. It takes time and effort to accumulate money. Often we lose sight of exactly whom we are providing for. Every child, in the safety of my office, says that they want more, not less, time with their parents. Children don't need "stuff," they need us: they need our inviting, listening presence.

3. *Materialism causes problems.* Materialistic kids have higher rates of emotional problems, fewer friends, and poorer grades than non-materialistic kids. Money is not what ratchets up rates of psychological problems; rather it is the culture of affluence—a culture that values things more than people, competition more than cooperation, and individuality more than reciprocity. All things being equal, affluent parents are more likely to capitulate to the culture of affluence, because their money makes this a readily available default setting.

It's not unusual for me to see a mother and daughter together in my office. Here's a typical visit. The girl is the queen bee at school—she's beautiful, bright, and sets the trends among peers.

To her great surprise and chagrin, she's just been dumped by her third boyfriend. She doesn't understand that the reason none of her boyfriends hang around for long is because she is so exhaustingly self-centered. As she cries in my office, her mom wraps an arm around her and says, "Don't worry, honey, we'll go shopping, you'll feel better." That's a parent who means well but who is not doing well for her child.

Every time we use a material thing as a way to calm a child, we rob that child of the opportunity to manage negative or unhappy feelings. Unhappy feelings are inevitable in life, and our kids need to learn how to navigate their way through challenges, disappointments, and unhappiness. We need to be teaching emotional resilience and self-management skills, not consumerism. We can suggest that the child call a friend, go for a walk, write in a diary, talk to a trusted teacher, and most importantly think about why she's having trouble holding on to her boyfriends. Teaching skills for managing unhappy feelings are good for a lifetime; designer outfits are only good for a season. . . .

An Alternative to Materialist Culture

Our materialist culture teaches us that if we only get our kids the right things—the right clothes, the right schools—that they will be happy. Our culture is wrong. The thrill that we get from "stuff" is amazingly short lived. Even lottery winners, people whose lives have been radically altered by great sums of money, have been found to return to the same level of happiness they were at before their windfall within about eight weeks.

Of course we want our children to be happy. But in order to successfully navigate through life, kids need more than happiness. They need a strong sense of self, an internal home, where they can retreat to problem solve and heal when the going gets tough. Even if we could give our children a "perfect" childhood—no unhappiness, no distress, no failure—we would be sadly mistaken if we thought that they would then have a "perfect" life. The notion of perfection is a childhood fantasy, one we would do well to get rid of. If every time our toddler fell, we picked him up, we would be

Teens of affluent parents feel disconnected from their parents more than any other socioeconomic group.

crippling him for life. He wouldn't learn how to fall down and find himself quite capable of getting up and starting out again. Every time we prematurely intervene for our children—call the teacher about a grade that doesn't seem right, or argue with the coach about why our child is sitting on the bench—we interfere with our child's ability to learn how to manage their own conflicts and disappointments. As our children grow, they carry themselves, not their parents, with them at all times.

The renowned pediatrician Dr. Spock said that a child who has not been bandaged has not been well loved. Part of being a parent is the very difficult job of watching our children struggle. It is an act of love that we are able to do this, and in the process we make sure that our children develop a healthy sense of self—the ability to be independent, capable, and connected to others.

Many children of privilege (as well as their parents) are disconnected and lonely. Our culture of materialism makes them lonelier, teaching them to replace people with things. They are vulnerable to the bankrupt values on TV shows like *My Supersweet Sixteen* or *Pimp My Ride*. Because of the pervasiveness of the media, we are all swimming in the same ocean of isolation and materialism. In that ocean, there is no safe harbor.

I've been on a book tour recently, and one day I found myself standing at the pulpit of an Episcopal church. It was awkward for a Jewish girl, accustomed to her home shul [synagogue], but I found my sense heightened by the newness of the situation. I started talking, and when I hit the part of my speech about how important it is for a child to be connected, I had a moment of intense clarity. I looked around at the people sitting in the pews and realized that you can't walk out on the street and create a community. You can't stand on a corner with a placard saying, "I'm ready to be connected to other people."

The church I was standing in—and other faith- or community-based institutions that embody parents' values—can provide that kind of ready-made community for our kids. They can be our safe harbors.

Children need communities where they can learn shared values and make connections that are not based on their performance. Children need places where people value them for being who they are, not for what they do or how they perform. They need parents who love them just for being themselves. They need a life in which the essence of a person matters, a life based on values. They need an inner life, a reflective life; they need, as we need, a more spiritual life.

FOUR

Teen Spending Habits Have Changed

Natalie Zmuda

> Natalie Zmuda, a retail reporter for *Advertising Age*, a magazine reporting on media and marketing news, discusses the global recession and the effect it has had on teen spending. Citing research and reports, she writes that while teens are cutting their spending on clothing, beauty, food, movies, and events like concerts, they have actually increased their spending on video games and game systems, music, and electronics such as the iPhone. She also says that teens today are aware of the economic downturn, that parents are likely to discuss household budgets with their teens, and that teens are showing empathy toward and receiving support from other teens in this difficult financial climate.

In a recession, one group can usually be counted on to keep spending: teens. Their parents often pick up the tab for necessities, leaving them free to spend the income they earn from part-time jobs and birthday money from grandma on themselves. But in this downturn, a rather surprising phenomenon is emerging: tight-fisted teens.

According to research from Piper Jaffray, teens are becoming more attuned to the pinch on household budgets from the economy, which is having a "dramatic impact" on the $125 billion

Natalie Zmuda, "Teens, Too, are Tightening Budgets," *Advertising Age*, April 27, 2009, p. 6. Copyright © 2009 Crain communications, Inc. Reproduced by permission.

the demographic spends each year. Teens generally have about $5,000 a year burning a hole in their pockets, but they are spending about 14% less this spring than in spring '08.

A study from Euro RSCG Discovery found that 92% of females ages 13 to 21 said they are at least somewhat worried about the economy, while 87% of males are. Teens are now asking themselves, "Do I need that?" and "Can I wait to have that?" Those are questions that historically have been of little concern to an age group that spent money as fast as they made it.

High Teen Unemployment

A grim unemployment picture for those ages 16 to 19 years old is also hampering spending. Unemployment rates in that age group have been rising, hitting nearly 22% in March [2009], the highest rate seen in more than a decade. The national average was 8.5% last month [March 2009]. "Teens, like their parents, are coming up against a tough job market. The standbys of restaurant and retail are trimming their ranks, not hiring," said Candace Corlett, president of WSL Strategic Retail, a consulting group. "It's going to be a tough summer for teens."

So what are they scrimping on? According to Piper Jaffray, they are cutting back on apparel, beauty and food, and excursions to movies, concerts and sporting events. Of course, there are limits: Teens are not willing to live without things such as music, DVDs, video games and video-game systems, and spending in those areas has been less affected.

Apple, Xbox and Electronic Arts can rest easy as can Nike and Starbucks.

Though apparel has seen one of the most dramatic declines in spending, slumping 22% year over year, teen spending on accessories is flat, and outlays on shoes have increased 4%, according to Piper Jaffray. The beauty category has seen a 12% decrease year over year.

iPhone the New Jean

Ellen Davis, VP at the National Retail Federation, said the recession has coincided with a sea change in teens' spending habits.

Teens (and adults) line up to purchase the latest must-have item for teens, the iPhone.

The latest gadgets have replaced trendy jeans and designer duds as must-haves. "Today's teens are so focused on communication that iPhones are becoming the new jean," she said.

Teens have also been trimming expenditures on eating out, spending some 20% less compared with fall 2007. Nicole Miller Regan, senior research analyst at Piper Jaffray, said one of the most interesting findings of the survey is the increasing importance of value to the group. Chipotle and McDonald's are gaining market share, though Starbucks remains the teen favorite.

"Key influencers have always been taste and convenience, but now value is trumping that," she said. "They're eating more at [quick-service restaurants] than they are at casual dining. It's all about value, value menus, dollar menus and a lower average ticket."

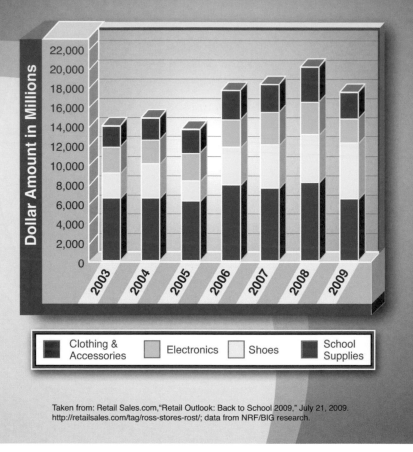

Total Projected Back-to-School Spending

Dollar Amount in Millions

22,000
20,000
18,000
16,000
14,000
12,000
10,000
8,000
6,000
4,000
2,000
0

2003 2004 2005 2006 2007 2008 2009

■ Clothing & Accessories ■ Electronics □ Shoes ■ School Supplies

Taken from: Retail Sales.com, "Retail Outlook: Back to School 2009," July 21, 2009.
http://retailsales.com/tag/ross-stores-rost/; data from NRF/BIG research.

Video Games, DVDs, and Music

There are a few bright spots, however. As a percentage of teen spending, video games have increased to 8% from 7% last spring. The Piper Jaffray study also found that teen gamers are far from price-sensitive, with 54% of all purchases ringing in at $50 or more. Music and DVDs also saw an increase to 11% of teens' budgets from 8% last spring, despite the rise of music and media downloading.

"Peer pressure is still peer pressure. When they're with their friends, they're not willing to cut back on things that give them a badge," said Zain Raj, CEO-Euro RSCG Discovery. "And spending on things that allow them to connect with their peer set are not as affected."

But, increasingly, teens are tuning in their parents, as opposed to tuning them out. Experts say teens are taking cues from parents who, even if they haven't been directly affected by the recession, are at least stressed. Many parents are also bringing the recession to the dinner table. A survey from CoolSavings, a division of Q Interactive, found that 84% of heads of household are discussing saving and budgeting with kids. And 81% say kids are aware of the recession and the impact it is having on household budgets. Kids are even beginning to pitch in, using coupons for things such as movies, music, museums and theme park trips, the survey found.

Today's Teens Are More Aware

That's in keeping with data WSL has cultivated showing teens are being more empathetic than apathetic. "It's startling. At the risk of stereotyping, we did see teens as sort of self-absorbed," said Ms. Corlett. "But teens are sensitive to what their parents are going through."

Today's teens are also more plugged in than their predecessors, a key differentiation from the recessions of the early 1980s, 1990s and, even, 2001. The rise of social networking has enabled teens to have hundreds of "friends" through services such as Facebook and Bebo. And that has made this recession much more personal for them.

"Teens have hundreds of friends on Facebook, so they're hearing about someone's dad losing his job or someone who has to move because their parent's company is downsizing," said Ms. Davis. "They're seeing the impact of the recession first-hand, even if it's someone they barely know."

FIVE

Rejecting Consumerism Is Beneficial

Amitai Etzioni

> Amitai Etzioni served as president of the American Sociological Association and is the author of *The Active Society*. In the following viewpoint, Etzioni asserts that consumerism has become a social disease that needs to be eradicated. Etzioni defines consumerism as the acquisition of goods and services to satisfy desires beyond basic human needs, such as food or shelter. Replacing the worship of consumer goods with communitarian pursuits or transcendental ones will improve society, he argues. While this is a change that will not occur overnight, he believes working to cut back on consumption will benefit America.

Much of the debate over how to address the economic crisis has focused on a single word: regulation. And it's easy to understand why. Bad behavior by a variety of businesses landed us in this mess—so it seems rather obvious that the way to avoid future economic meltdowns is to create, and vigorously enforce, new rules proscribing such behavior. But the truth is quite a bit more complicated. The world economy consists of billions of transactions every day. There can never be enough inspectors, accountants, customs officers, and police to ensure that all or even most of these transactions are properly carried out.

Amitai Etzioni, "Spent: America After Consumerism," *The New Republic*, June 17, 2009. Reproduced by permission of *The New Republic*.

Moreover, those charged with enforcing regulations are themselves not immune to corruption, and, hence, they too must be supervised and held accountable to others—who also have to be somehow regulated. The upshot is that regulation cannot be the linchpin of attempts to reform our economy. What is needed instead is something far more sweeping: for people to internalize a different sense of how one ought to behave, and act on it because they believe it is right.

That may sound far-fetched. It is commonly believed that people conduct themselves in a moral manner mainly because they fear the punishment that will be meted out if they engage in anti-social behavior. But this position does not stand up to close inspection. Most areas of behavior are extralegal; we frequently do what is expected because we care or love. This is evident in the ways we attend to our children (beyond a very low requirement set by law), treat our spouses, do volunteer work, and participate in public life. What's more, in many of those areas that are covered by law, the likelihood of being caught is actually quite low, and the penalties are often surprisingly mild. For instance, only about one in 100 tax returns gets audited, and most cheaters are merely asked to pay back what they "missed," plus some interest. Nevertheless, most Americans pay the taxes due. Alan Lewis's classic study *The Psychology of Taxation* concluded that people don't just pay taxes because they fear the government; they do it because they consider the burden fairly shared and the monies legitimately spent. In short, the normative values of a culture matter. Regulation is needed when culture fails, but it cannot alone serve as the mainstay of good conduct.

Eradicating Consumerism

So what kind of transformation in our normative culture is called for? What needs to be eradicated, or at least greatly tempered, is consumerism: the obsession with acquisition that has become the organizing principle of American life. This is not the same thing as capitalism, nor is it the same thing as consumption. To explain the difference, it is useful to draw on

Rejecting Consumerism Is Beneficial

Selected Religious Perspectives on Consumption

Faith	Perspective
Bahá'í' Faith	"In all matters moderation is desirable. If a thing is carried to excess, it will prove a source of evil." (Bahá'u'lláh, *Tablets of Bahá'u'lláh*)
Buddhism	"Whoever in this world overcomes his selfish cravings, his sorrow fall away from him, like drops of water from a lotus flower." (Dhammapada, 336)
Christianity	"No one can be the slave of two masters....You cannot be the slave both of God and money." (Matthew, 6:24)
Confucianism	"Excess and deficiency are equally at fault." (Confucious)
Hinduism	"That person who lives completely free from desires, without longing...attains that peace." (Bhagavad Gita, 11)
Islam	"Eat and drink, but waste not by excess: He loves not the excessive." (Qu'ran, 7.31)
Judaism	"Give me neither poverty nor riches." (Proverbs, 30:8)
Taoism	"He who knows he has enough is rich." (*Tao Te Ching*)

Taken from: Gary Gardner, "Engaging Religions to Shape Worldviews." In 2010 *State of the World: Transforming Cultures; From Consumerism to Sustainability,* edited by Worldwatch Institute, pp. 23-29. New York: Norton, 2010.

Abraham Maslow's hierarchy of human needs. At the bottom of this hierarchy are basic creature comforts; once these are sated, more satisfaction is drawn from affection, self-esteem, and, finally, self-actualization. As long as consumption is focused on satisfying basic human needs—safety, shelter, food, clothing, health care, education—it is not consumerism. But, when the acquisition of goods and services is used to satisfy the higher needs, consumption turns into consumerism—and consumerism becomes a social disease.

The link to the economic crisis should be obvious. A culture in which the urge to consume dominates the psychology of citizens is a culture in which people will do most anything to acquire the means to consume—working slavish hours, behaving rapaciously in their business pursuits, and even bending the rules in order to maximize their earnings. They will also buy homes beyond their means and think nothing of running up credit-card debt. It therefore seems safe to say that consumerism is, as much as anything else, responsible for the current economic mess. But it is not enough to establish that which people ought not to do, to end the obsession with making and consuming evermore than the next person. Consumerism will not just magically disappear from its central place in our culture. It needs to be supplanted by *something*.

A shift away from consumerism, and toward this something else, would obviously be a dramatic change for American society. But such grand cultural changes are far from unprecedented.

To accomplish this kind of radical change, it is neither necessary nor desirable to imitate devotees of the 1960s counterculture, early socialists, or followers of ascetic religious orders, all of whom have resisted consumerism by rejecting the whole capitalist project. On the contrary, capitalism should be allowed to thrive, albeit within clear and well-enforced limits. This position does not call for a life of sackcloth and ashes, nor of altruism. And it does not call on poor people or poor nations to be content with their fate and learn to love their misery; clearly, the capitalist economy must be strong enough to provide for the basic creature comforts of all people. But it does call for a new balance between consumption and other human pursuits.

There is strong evidence that when consumption is used to try to address higher needs—that is, needs beyond basic creature comforts—it is ultimately Sisyphean. Several studies have shown that, across many nations with annual incomes above $20,000, there is no correlation between increased income and increased happiness. In the United States since World War II, per capita income has tripled, but levels of life satisfaction remain about the same, while the people of Japan, despite experiencing a sixfold increase in income since 1958, have seen their levels of contentment stay largely stagnant. Studies also indicate that many members of capitalist societies feel unsatisfied, if not outright deprived, however much they earn and consume, because others make and spend even more: Relative rather than absolute deprivation is what counts. This is a problem since, by definition, most people cannot consume more than most others. True, it is sometimes hard to tell a basic good from a status good, and a status good can turn into a basic one (air conditioning, for instance). However, it is not a matter of cultural snobbery to note that no one *needs* inflatable Santas or plastic flamingos on their front lawn or, for that matter, lawns that are strikingly green even in the scorching heat of summer. No one needs a flat-screen television, not to mention diamonds as a token of love or a master's painting as a source of self-esteem.

Consumerism Afflicts Many Americans

Consumerism, it must be noted, afflicts not merely the upper class in affluent societies but also the middle class and many in the working class. Large numbers of people across society believe that they work merely to make ends meet, but an examination of their shopping lists and closets reveals that they spend good parts of their income on status goods such as brand-name clothing, the "right" kind of car, and other assorted items that they don't really need.

This mentality may seem so integral to American culture that resisting it is doomed to futility. But the current economic downturn may provide an opening of sorts. The crisis has caused people to spend less on luxury goods, such as diamonds and flashy cars; scale back on lavish celebrations for holidays, birthdays, weddings, and bar mitzvahs; and agree to caps on executive compensation. Some workers have accepted fewer hours, lower salaries, and unpaid furloughs.

So far, much of this scaling-back has been involuntary, the result of economic necessity. What is needed next is to help people realize that limiting consumption is not a reflection of failure. Rather, it represents liberation from an obsession—a chance to abandon consumerism and focus on . . . well, what exactly? What should replace the worship of consumer goods?

The kind of culture that would best serve a Maslowian hierarchy of needs is hardly one that would kill the goose that lays the golden eggs—the economy that can provide the goods needed for basic creature comforts. Nor one that merely mocks the use of consumer goods to respond to higher needs. It must be a culture that extols sources of human flourishing besides acquisition. The two most obvious candidates to fill this role are communitarian pursuits and transcendental ones.

Communitarianism refers to investing time and energy in relations with the other, including family, friends, and members of one's community. The term also encompasses service to the common good, such as volunteering, national service, and politics. Communitarian life is not centered around altruism but around mutuality, in the sense that deeper and thicker involvement with the other is rewarding to both the recipient and the giver. Indeed, numerous studies show that communitarian pursuits breed deep contentment. A study of 50-year-old men shows that those with friendships are far less likely to experience heart disease. Another shows that life satisfaction in older adults is higher for those who participate in community service.

Transcendental pursuits refer to spiritual activities broadly understood, including religious, contemplative, and artistic ones. The lifestyle of the Chinese literati, centered around poetry, philosophy, and brush painting, was a case in point, but a limited one because this lifestyle was practiced by an elite social stratum and based in part on exploitation of other groups. In modern society, transcendental pursuits have often been emphasized by bohemians, beginning artists, and others involved in lifelong learning who consume modestly. Here again, however, these people make up only a small fraction of society. Clearly, for a culture to buy out of consumerism and move to satisfying higher human needs with transcendental projects, the option to participate in these pursuits must be available on a wider scale.

Moving Beyond Consumerism

All this may seem abstract, not to mention utopian. But one can see a precedent of sorts for a society that emphasizes communitarian and transcendental pursuits among retired people, who spend the final decades of their lives painting not for a market or galleries but as a form of self-expression, socializing with each other,

Actor and writer Robert Llewellyn writes of his yearlong effort not to buy anything new in his effort to reject consumerism.

volunteering, and, in some cases, taking classes. Of course, these citizens already put in the work that enables them to lead this kind of life. For other ages to participate before retirement, they will have to shorten their workweek and workday, refuse to take work home, turn off their BlackBerrys, and otherwise downgrade the centrality of labor to their lives. This is, in effect, what the French, with their 35-hour workweeks, tried to do, as did other countries in "old" Europe. Mainstream American economists—who argue that a modern economy cannot survive unless people consume evermore and hence produce and work evermore—have long scoffed at these societies and urged them to modernize. To some extent, they did, especially the Brits. Now it seems that maybe these countries were onto something after all.

Is all this an idle, abstract hypothesis? Not necessarily. Plenty of religious Americans have already embraced versions of these values to some extent or other. And those whose secular beliefs lead them to community service are in the same boat. One such idealist named Barack Obama chose to be a community organizer in Chicago rather than pursue a more lucrative career.

I certainly do not expect that most people will move away from a consumerist mindset overnight. Some may keep one foot in the old value system even as they test the waters of the new one, just like those who wear a blazer with jeans. Still others may merely cut back on conspicuous consumption without guilt or fear of social censure. Societies shift direction gradually. All that is needed is for more and more people to turn the current economic crisis into a liberation from the obsession with consumer goods and the uberwork it requires—and, bit by bit, begin to rethink their definition of what it means to live a good life.

SIX

Rejecting Consumerism Is Not Realistic

Tim Cavanaugh

In this viewpoint, written in the spring of 2009, Tim Cavanaugh, a columnist for *Reason* magazine, explores what the critics of consumer culture and advocates of voluntary simplicity must be thinking about the recession, wondering, tongue-in-cheek, if they are ecstatic about it. He reports on the three coauthors of the 2001 book *Affluenza: The All-Consuming Epidemic* and how they view the current economic times. One author says, "I'm sorry that it happened this way." Another now supports President Barack Obama's American Recovery and Reinvestment Act, because he does not want "the whole ship to sink." The third author is now working for the political independence of Vermont and says that in the long run the current collapse of the global market will not be a bad thing.

If there's a silver lining in the clouds over the global economy, Live Simplers are the people you'd expect to find it.

Proponents of voluntary simplicity, critics of excessive consumption, localists, sustainability advocates, and other mild-mannered critics of consumer culture have a lot to brag on these days. They have stooped for years under the tyranny of big-box retailers, SUVs, wall-sized televisions, crap culture, gourmet coffees, and self-storage facilities.

Consumerism and the New Economy

And here it all is going tits up, just as the Live Simplers knew it would. Greedy financiers, scheming money-lenders, and ignorant American fatsos are all getting their comeuppance, oozing bad debt, punished for living beyond their means. Affluenza has been cured. Its related ailments—shopoholism, work-life imbalance, expenditure cascades, status anxiety, positional externalities—are in remission.

What political faction can claim a win this vast? Libertarians are finding few takers for arguments against market intervention. Social justice types must explain away the redistributionist antics of Fannie Mae and Freddie Mac. Only the Live Simplers can say with straight faces that they told us so. But gloating has never been their style.

Affluenza is a term psychologists give for an excessive desire to consume material goods.

"I'm sorry that it happened this way," says John de Graaf, national coordinator of the Take Back Your Time campaign and one of the authors of *Affluenza: The All-Consuming Epidemic*, a 2001 book based on a late-'90s public television documentary. "I'm not riding high thinking this is a great thing. I would rather see us wean ourselves gradually than have it go off like a bomb."

A Broad Critique

That more-sorrow-than-anger spirit sets the Live Simplers apart from their occasional bedfellows, the hardcore Collapsitarians, who are generally excited to see the whole mother burn to the ground. Yet it's the Live Simplers who have contributed the most context to the current mood. If, for example, you have recently been emailed the popular "What the World Eats" photo essay—juxtaposing pictures of American and European families and their weekly food supplies with pictures of fancifully garbed families in Bhutan, Chad, and other distant, underfed lands—you're seeing a trick essentially drawn from *Affluenza*. The genius of the simplicity movement was to shape a political argument (an extraordinarily broad and total critique of commercial exchange) into a spiritual koan [a riddle or puzzle] (why am I so unfulfilled by my Big Macs and gadgets when simple Bushmen have all the soul nourishment they need?).

A vision that broad, however, turns out to be difficult to follow to its logical conclusion. David Wann, president of the Sustainable Futures Society and one of De Graaf's two co-authors on *Affluenza*, describes the overstimulated economy of the post-Reagan era as a "completely toxic loaf," yet he also supports the American Recovery and Reinvestment Act's $550 billion economic stimulus component—both because more than $100 billion of that spending is targeted at environmental-ish initiatives and because "we don't want the whole ship to sink."

Why so squeamish? De Graaf cites humanitarian concerns. "The enormous expectations in the American economy, unmatched by increases in real wages, and the gap between the rich and poor, all led to this crisis," he says. "Even I would not have predicted it

"... so I decided to make us all fabulous new outfits from the Guardian environment supplement!"

Cartoon by Clive Goddard, www.CartoonStock.com.

would be as extreme as it is. I didn't think it would be this high a price. This crisis is horribly painful for people."

Involuntary Simplicity

That's an understandable concern, but then, what is to be done? If ending hyperconsumption was impossible in boom times, and belt tightening imposed by hard fiscal reality doesn't count because it's not voluntary simplicity, then how do you ever move masses of men to change their lives of quiet desperation?

And given that even during the boom few of us could spend $95 on a sea grass market basket or $145 on a Holy Lamb Organics diaper-changing pad, is radical economic change the best path to sustainability? President Obama plans to spend $31 billion just for green retrofitting of government buildings. Experience suggests that simplicity or localism at anything more than boutique scale is expensive. McMansions and PDAs (which are available in the grimmest developing-world hellholes) may or may not be excrescences of an overstimulated economy. But public libraries and organic farmers markets definitely are.

The third author of *Affluenza* has taken a path decidedly different from his colleagues'. Thomas H. Naylor, who now dismisses the work as a "cutesy book," founded the Second Vermont Republic (SVR) in 2003. This separatist movement works for "political independence for Vermont and the peaceful dissolution of the Union." The SVR's goals include "Human Scale, Sustainability, Tension Reduction," etc., but its rhetoric has a febrile, hot-medium quality that you wouldn't normally associate with the Green Mountain State.

Naylor freely disparages the new administration ("if anything, Obama's worse, because he's smarter than Bush, and better able to sell that") and draws a hard moral about the collapse of the global market ("technofascism carried to its logical conclusion: robotism, megalomania, globalization, and imperialism"). He is also sanguine about the market's rough justice. "In the long run, it's not going to be bad news," says Naylor. "The global economy will be radically different under Obama, but he had little to do with changing it. This is the death spiral of the global economy."

Simplicity Is Not About Money

That's still a hard conceptual leap for most Live Simplers to make. "Although some religious traditions have advocated a life of extreme renunciation," wrote Duane Elgin in his 1981 book *Voluntary Simplicity: Toward a Way of Life That Is Outwardly Simple, Inwardly Rich*, "it is inaccurate to equate simplicity with poverty." The Live Simplers seek a change not in people's fortunes but in their hearts, and that's a recipe for eternal disappointment. "Affluenza hasn't been solved," says Wann, "because there's still this assumption that now we're down, but as soon as we can we'll get back up again."

SEVEN

High Socioeconomic Status Causes Depression

Peter Dodson

Writing for *Briarpatch*, an independent Canadian bimonthly current-issues magazine, Peter Dodson, a researcher, writer, and teacher, draws a correlation between materialism and depression. Dodson cites statistics indicating the high and growing rates of depression and suicide in modern consumer societies. He also quotes researchers who believe that increased financial success does not increase happiness but in fact causes illness, stress, and depression. Furthermore, he explains that this depression is a natural body reaction and warning signal that consumerism is harmful and is best treated by natural methods such as increased exercise, better sleep, and community activities.

Of all the notions by which our society abides, none influences our daily life more than the idea that "money buys happiness." It is why Canadians spend an average of 8.9 hours a day working, up from 8.4 hours just 20 years ago. It is why we forfeited 32 million vacation days last year and have over $750 billion in debt. It is why we average 12 full days per year commuting to and from work. But if happiness is what we're after, there's a growing body of evidence that suggests we're on a dead-end path. While our houses get bigger and our televisions become wider, flatter,

Peter Dodson, "Buying Happiness: The Depressing Reality of Materialism," *Briarpatch*, September/ October 2007, pp. 21–22. Reproduced by permission.

more colourful and cheaper, greater numbers of us are becoming depressed.

Perhaps one of the deepest, darkest secrets of industrial society is that despite rising income, levels of depression are at an all-time high. In a 2006 report published by the Centre for Economic Performance at the London School of Economics, "According to the respected Psychiatric Morbidity Survey, [if testing were universal,] one in six of us would be diagnosed as having depression or chronic anxiety disorder, which means that one family in three is affected." The Ontario Ministry of Health Promotion's Healthy Ontario website states that "At any given time, almost three million Canadians have serious depression." In other words, around ten percent of Canadians are currently suffering from serious depression.

An Epidemic of Depression

These numbers are alarming on their own, but when we take into account the fact that since the end of World War II the rates of major depressive disorders have increased tenfold, it is clear that the problem is much more serious than many of us realize. The rates are increasing so rapidly that the World Health Organization has predicted that depression will be the second leading cause of death and disability worldwide by 2020, largely due to undiagnosed depression—a leading cause of suicide that is becoming an epidemic in its own right.

Last year [2006], the American television news program *Dateline* featured a report on a lawyer from Toronto who had an incurable form of depression, one that had not been made better by antidepressants, psychotherapy, or even extensive electroshock therapy. Throughout the piece, the reporter commented that the lawyer "had it all," implying that her affluence and comfort made it all the more confusing why she had depression in the first place, let alone why it was so extreme. The assumption, of course, is that people who have a high standard of living, with the requisite happy family and abundant material goods, should be happy. Not once did the reporter, the patient, her husband, or any of the doctors suggest (or perhaps even consider) that the problem might actually be precisely that she "had it all" in the first place.

While money and material goods afford people a comfortable standard of living, they in no way guarantee one a happy life. In his paper "The Economics of Happiness," Richard Easterlin, a professor of economics well known for his work in this area, found that even though his research subjects had more than doubled their income over a 28-year period, it did not make them any happier. Indeed, as Bill McKibben reports in the March/April 2007 issue of *Mother Jones*, income only correlates with happiness until the point where a person's basic needs are met (about $10,000 per year). After that point, increases in income simply do not correlate to increased well-being: "The 'life satisfaction' of pavement dwellers—homeless people—in Calcutta is among the lowest recorded," McKibben writes, "but it almost doubles when they move into a slum, at which point they are basically as satisfied with their lives as a sample of college students drawn from 47 nations."

Materialism and Depression

Not only does more money not generally translate into greater happiness, but researchers like Tim Kasser and Juliet Schor have shown that the intense pursuit of wealth and material goods can actually make a person ill. In *Born to Buy*, Schor's work with "tweens" (children between 8 and 12) showed that "The more they buy into the consumer materialist messages, the worse they feel about themselves, the more depressed they are, and the more they are beset by anxiety, headaches, stomach aches and boredom." Kasser's studies have borne similar results, and he concludes in his book, *The High Price of Materialism*, that "when people follow materialistic values and organize their lives around attaining wealth and possessions, they are essentially wasting their time as far as well-being is concerned." It would seem that while striving to live like Oprah may seem a good idea, it could have tragic mental health consequences.

But why are people more at risk for problems like depression the more they embrace materialism? One of the major reasons is

"I NEED ANOTHER RAISE SO I CAN PAY FOR THE CAR I BOUGHT TO CELEBRATE MY LAST RAISE."

"Asking for a Raise," cartoon by Edgar Argo. www.CartoonStock.com.

that materialistic people tend to participate in activities like shopping, watching television and mindlessly surfing the Internet that do not give them much emotional, mental, or physical benefit. While buying a luxury item might give someone a short burst of joy or satisfaction, consumption does not make us happy for very long because, as we all know, there is always something new to buy—something else that we just have to have. Not only do materialistic people engage in activities that do little for their well-being, but while they pursue these activities they ignore more important behaviours such as socializing with others, exercising, participating in community events, and just plain being active for the fun of it rather than to earn (or spend) a buck.

Materialism and Stress

The trends speak for themselves: Canadians are working 30 minutes longer and spending 45 minutes less time with family on an average workday than they did 20 years ago. We are also increasingly eating alone, watching television alone, and spending less time preparing meals. In a 2006 study published in the *Washington Post*, it was found that a quarter of all Americans said that they have "no one with whom they can discuss personal troubles." If the experts are correct and we require human contact to maintain our mental health, all of these trends suggest that we are moving in the wrong direction.

Not only does consumer culture encourage us to engage in activities contrary to our well-being and avoid other, more beneficial activities, but it also causes us a great deal of stress—one of the key triggers of a depressive episode. Keeping up with the Joneses—not to mention the Hiltons—requires that people spend long hours at demanding and stressful jobs, skip holidays and needed sleep, and amass record amounts of debt in order to have the latest fashions. As well, the ideals that television and advertising present, in terms of aesthetics and emotional well-being, are so far beyond the means of average people that many end up feeling bad about themselves for not living up to those ideals—but that does not stop them from trying. The result can be lowered self-esteem and a reduced sense of well-being.

Depression as a Warning

While mental health professionals have traditionally looked at depression as a result of either genetic, biochemical, or environmental factors, some evolutionary theorists are now looking at depression in a much different light. Randolph Nesse of the University of Michigan has argued that, like pain, depression and depressive symptoms serve the adaptive function of stopping humans from engaging in activities that are harmful to them or of little benefit. In a 2000 article entitled "Is Depression an Adaptation?" Nesse argued that "some negative and passive aspects of depression may be useful because they inhibit dangerous and wasteful actions in situations characterized by committed pursuit of an unreachable goal, temptations to challenge authority, insufficient internal reserves to allow action without damage, or lack of a viable life strategy." In a 2006 study with Matthew Keller,

Nesse also found that certain negative situations aroused particular depressive symptoms. They found that people who were engaged in "failing efforts" were stricken with depressive symptoms such as "guilt, rumination, pessimism, and fatigue," leading them to conclude that these reactions "may have been shaped by natural selection to minimize wasted effort and to re-assess failing strategies."

The question needs to be asked, then: Are rates of depression rising because our bodies are reacting naturally to discourage us from engaging in a consumer culture that is not delivering on its promise? The research of Kasser and Schor, which shows that people highly involved in material culture are more prone to depression, along with that of evolutionary theorists like Nesse, suggests that this may indeed be the case. Instead of examining the effects of overconsumption and suburbia on our mental health, however, modern society has so far dealt with the depression epidemic by introducing another commodity: antidepressants. While antidepressants can be effective at treating the symptoms of the problem, they do nothing to address deeper factors influencing depression, such as diet, a lack of exercise, and stress. If depression is the body's way of warning us to stop engaging in harmful behaviour, suppressing the symptoms with drugs only encourages us to ignore our built-in warning system, and ultimately, ignore the reasons why we are depressed in the first place.

Anti-consumerism as an Antidote

Fortunately, the toll the consumerist lifestyle takes on our mental health and well-being need not be permanent. Stephen Ilardi, a University of Kansas psychologist, has shown that when people actually change their habits through a method he calls "therapeutic lifestyle change," they have a better chance of treating their depression than those using medication and therapy. In a February 12, 2007, *Los Angeles Times* article, Ilardi argued that human beings were not designed "for our sedentary, socially isolated, indoor, sleep-deprived, frenzied, poorly nourished lifestyle"—in short, the modern consumer world. His treatment method has people exercise more, sleep more, eat

Keeping up with the Joneses requires many to spend long hours at stressful jobs and to amass record debt in the pursuit of material things.

more Omega-3's, and, finally, interact more with their fellow human beings. The results have been stunning: "in an on-going study of 79 patients, with two-thirds assigned to his therapy and the rest to a control group treated mainly with antidepressant medication or traditional psychotherapy, Ilardi reports a 74 percent favorable response, compared with 16 percent for the controls." Just like a child learns to avoid or reduce pain by removing her finger from a candle flame, there is hope yet that we can turn the depression epidemic around by unplugging from the consumerist model and pursuing more fruitful ambitions.

EIGHT

Advertising Is to Blame for Overconsumption

Jean Kilbourne

Jean Kilbourne, an author, speaker, and filmmaker, is a cultural critic who frequently speaks out about the negative impact of advertising on individuals and society. Writing here for the *New Internationalist*, a magazine that reports on world poverty and inequality, she discusses the effect of current advertising campaigns and their trend to promise personal transformation via material objects. Citing examples, she notes that advertisements have shifted from promising better relationships with others because of what we buy to promising fulfilling relationships with the things themselves. She also explains the concept of propaganda and the irony that advertising works so well because we believe that it does not affect us.

A recent ad for Thule car-rack systems features a child in the backseat of a car, seatbelt on. Next to the child, assorted sporting gear is carefully strapped into a child's carseat. The headline says: "We Know What Matters to You." In case one misses the point, further copy adds: "Your gear is a priority."

Another ad features an attractive young couple in bed. The man is on top of the woman, presumably making love to her. However, her face is completely covered by a magazine, open to a double-page photo of a car. The man is gazing passionately at the car. The copy reads, "The ultimate attraction."

These ads are meant to be funny. Taken individually, I suppose they might seem amusing or, at worst, tasteless. As someone who has studied ads for a long time, however, I see them as part of a pattern: just two of many ads that state or imply that products are more important than people. Ads have long promised us a better relationship via a product: *buy this and you will be loved.* But more recently they have gone beyond that proposition to promise us a relationship with the product itself: *buy this and it will love you.* The product is not so much the means to an end, as the end itself.

After all, it is easier to love a product than a person. Relationships with human beings are messy, unpredictable, sometimes dangerous. "When was the last time you felt this comfortable in a relationship?" asks an ad for shoes. Our shoes never ask us to wash the dishes or tell us we're getting fat. Even more important, products don't betray us. "You can love it without getting your heart broken," proclaims a car ad. One certainly can't say that about loving a human being, as love without vulnerability is impossible.

We are surrounded by hundreds, thousands of messages every day that link our deepest emotions to products, that objectify people and trivialize our most heartfelt moments and relationships. Every emotion is used to sell us something. Our wish to protect our children is leveraged to make us buy an expensive car. A long marriage simply provides the occasion for a diamond necklace. A painful reunion between a father and his estranged daughter is dramatized to sell us a phone system. Everything in the world—nature, animals, people—is just so much stuff to be consumed or to be used to sell us something.

The problem with advertising isn't that it creates artificial needs, but that it exploits our very real and human desires. Advertising promotes a bankrupt concept of *relationship.* Most of us yearn for committed relationships that will last. We are not stupid: we know that buying a certain brand of cereal won't bring us one inch closer to that goal. But we are surrounded by advertising that yokes our needs with products and promises us that *things*

Americans are bombarded every day with thousands of advertisements that use every technique to make us want to buy, buy, buy.

deliver what in fact they never can. In the world of advertising, lovers are things and things are lovers.

It may be that there is no other way to depict relationships when the ultimate goal is to sell products. But this apparently bottomless consumerism not only depletes the world's resources, it also depletes our inner resources. It leads inevitably to narcissism and solipsism [selfishness and egotism]. It becomes difficult to imagine a way of relating that isn't objectifying and exploitative.

Tuned In

Most people feel that advertising is not something to take seriously. Other aspects of the media are serious—the violent films, the trashy talk shows, the bowdlerization [simplification] of the news. But not advertising! Although much more attention has been paid to the cultural impact of advertising in recent years than ever before, just about everyone still feels personally exempt from its influence. What I hear more than anything else at my lectures is: "I don't pay attention to ads . . . I just tune them out . . . they have no effect on me." I hear this most from people wearing clothes emblazoned with logos. In truth, we are all influenced. There is no way to tune out this much information, especially when it is designed to break through the "tuning out" process. As advertising critic Sut Jhally put it: "To not be influenced by advertising would be to live outside of culture. No human being lives outside of culture."

Much of advertising's power comes from this belief that it does not affect us. As Joseph Goebbels said: "This is the secret of propaganda: those who are to be persuaded by it should be completely immersed in the ideas of the propaganda, without ever noticing that they are being immersed in it." Because we think advertising is trivial, we are less on guard, less critical, than we might otherwise be. While we're laughing, sometimes sneering, the commercial does its work.

Taken individually, ads are silly, sometimes funny, certainly nothing to worry about. But cumulatively they create a climate of cynicism that is poisonous to relationships. Ad after ad portrays our real lives as dull and ordinary, commitment to human beings as something to be avoided. Because of the pervasiveness of this kind of message, we learn from childhood that it is far safer to make a commitment to a product than to a person, far easier to be loyal to a brand. Many end up feeling romantic about material objects yet deeply cynical about other human beings.

Unnatural Passions

We know by now that advertising often turns people into objects. Women's bodies—and men's bodies too these days—are dismembered, packaged and used to sell everything from chainsaws to chewing gum, champagne to shampoo. Self-image is deeply affected. The self-esteem of girls plummets as they reach adolescence partly because they cannot possibly escape the message that their bodies are objects, and imperfect objects at that. Boys learn that masculinity requires a kind of ruthlessness, even brutality.

Advertising encourages us not only to objectify each other but to feel passion for products rather than our partners. This is especially dangerous when the products are potentially addictive, because addicts do feel they are in a relationship with their substances. I once heard an alcoholic joke that Jack Daniels was her most constant lover. When I was a smoker, I felt that my cigarettes were my friends. Advertising reinforces these beliefs, so we are twice seduced—by the ads and by the substances themselves.

The addict is the ideal consumer. Ten per cent of drinkers consume over sixty per cent of all the alcohol sold. Most of them are alcoholics or people in desperate trouble—but they are also the alcohol industry's very best customers. Advertisers spend enormous amounts of money on psychological research and understand addiction well. They use this knowledge to target children (because if you hook them early they are yours for life), to encourage all people to consume more, in spite of often dangerous consequences for all of us, and to create a climate of denial in which all kinds of addictions flourish. This they do with full intent, as we see so clearly in the "secret documents" of the tobacco industry that have been made public in recent years.

The consumer culture encourages us not only to buy more but to seek our identity and fulfillment through what we buy, to express our individuality through our "choices" of products. Advertising corrupts relationships and then offers us products, both as solace and as substitutes for the intimate human connection we all long for and need.

In the world of advertising, lovers grow cold, spouses grow old, children grow up and away—but possessions stay with us and never change. Seeking the outcomes of a healthy relationship through products cannot work. Sometimes it leads us into addiction. But at best the possessions can never deliver the promised goods. They can't make us happy or loved or less alone or safe. If we believe they can, we are doomed to disappointment. No matter how much we love them, they will never love us back.

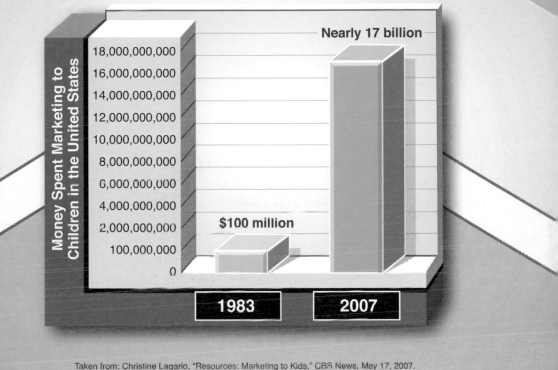

Money Spent Marketing Products to Children in the United States Has Increased Dramatically

Money Spent Marketing to Children in the United States

- 18,000,000,000
- 16,000,000,000
- 14,000,000,000
- 12,000,000,000
- 10,000,000,000
- 8,000,000,000
- 6,000,000,000
- 4,000,000,000
- 2,000,000,000
- 100,000,000
- 0

Nearly 17 billion

$100 million

1983 | 2007

Taken from: Christine Lagario, "Resources: Marketing to Kids," CBS News, May 17, 2007. wwwcbsnews.com/stories/2007/05/14/fyl/main2798401.shtml.

Some argue that advertising simply reflects societal values rather than affecting them. Far from being a passive mirror of society, however, advertising is a pervasive medium of influence and persuasion. Its influence is cumulative, often subtle and primarily unconscious. A former editor-in-chief of *Advertising Age*, the leading advertising publication in North America, once claimed: "Only eight per cent of an ad's message is received by the conscious mind. The rest is worked and re-worked deep within, in the recesses of the brain."

Advertising performs much the same function in industrial society as myth did in ancient societies. It is both a creator and perpetuator of the dominant values of the culture, the social norms by which most people govern their behaviour. At the very least, advertising helps to create a climate in which certain values flourish and others are not reflected at all.

Advertising is not only our physical environment, it is increasingly our spiritual environment as well. By definition, however, it is only interested in materialistic values. When spiritual values show up in ads, it is only in order to sell us something. Eternity is a perfume by Calvin Klein. Infiniti is an automobile, and Hydra Zen a moisturizer. Jesus is a brand of jeans.

Sometimes the allusion is more subtle, as in the countless alcohol ads featuring the bottle surrounded by a halo of light. Indeed products such as jewellery shining in a store window are often displayed as if they were sacred objects. Advertising co-opts our sacred symbols in order to evoke an immediate emotional response. Media critic Neil Postman referred to this as "cultural rape."

It is commonplace to observe that consumerism has become the religion of our time (with advertising its holy text), but the criticism usually stops short of what is at the heart of the comparison. Both advertising and religion share a belief in transformation, but most religions believe that this requires sacrifice. In the world of advertising, enlightenment is achieved instantly by purchasing material goods. An ad for a watch says, "It's not your handbag. It's not your neighbourhood. It's not your boyfriend. It's your watch that tells most about who you are." Of course, this cheapens authentic spirituality and transcendence. This junk food for the soul leaves us hungry, empty, malnourished.

Substitute Stories

Human beings used to be influenced primarily by the stories of our particular tribe or community, not by stories that are mass-produced and market-driven. As George Gerbner, one of the world's most respected researchers on the influence of the media, said: "For the first time in human history, most of the stories about people, life and values are told not by parents, schools, churches, or others in the community who have something to tell, but by a group of distant conglomerates that have something to sell."

Although it is virtually impossible to measure the influence of advertising on a culture, we can learn something by looking at cultures only recently exposed to it. In 1980 the Gwich'in tribe of Alaska got television, and therefore massive advertising, for the first time. Satellite dishes, video games and VCRs were not far behind. Before this, the Gwich'in lived much the way their ancestors had for generations. Within 10 years, the young members of the tribe were so drawn by television they no longer had time to learn ancient hunting methods, their parents' language or their oral history. Legends told around campfires could not compete with *Beverly Hills 90210*. Beaded moccasins gave way to Nike sneakers, and "tundra tea" to Folger's instant coffee.

As multinational chains replace local character, we end up in a world in which everyone is Gapped and Starbucked. Shopping malls kill vibrant downtown centres locally and create a universe of uniformity internationally. We end up in a world ruled by, in [economist] John Maynard Keynes's phrase, the values of the casino. On this deeper level, rampant commercialism undermines our physical and psychological health, our environment and our civic life, and creates a toxic society.

Advertising creates a world view that is based upon cynicism, dissatisfaction and craving. Advertisers aren't evil. They are just doing their job, which is to sell a product; but the consequences, usually unintended, are often destructive. In the history of the world there has never been a propaganda effort to match that of advertising in the past 50 years. More thought, more effort, more money goes into advertising than has gone into any other campaign to change social consciousness. The story that advertising tells is that the way to be happy, to find satisfaction—and the path to political freedom, as well—is through the consumption of material objects. And the major motivating force for social change throughout the world today is this belief that happiness comes from the market.

NINE

Human Instinct Is to Blame for Overconsumption

John Naish

Increasingly, members of western society seem to be aware that they have an overabundance of possessions yet still find it difficult not to buy more things than they need. John Naish, lifestyle writer for the *Times* and author of *Enough: Breaking Free from the World of More*, writes here for the *Ecologist*, explaining some biological reasons for this phenomenon. Citing scientific studies, he writes that due to the scarcity experienced by ancient ancestors, human brains are hardwired always to desire more than what is at hand. While advertising plays into the way people behave, it is not the direct cause of overconsumption.

Ever since the 1970s we have lived with the growing awareness that our ecosystem is fragile and the perpetual exploitation of our natural resources impossible. By the late 1980s, even *The Sun* newspaper had its own green correspondent. Everything we buy, use and throw away has an impact somewhere on the ecological continuum, and nowadays the most bullish Western consumers' consciences are regularly punctured by shards of eco-worry. We also increasingly realise that working ever harder for more possessions, more options, more stuff, doesn't tend to make us more content. Instead it can cause anxiety, stress and depression. Lifestyle pundits blame "society" or the Government. Some say

John Naish, "Born to Shop?" *The Ecologist*, February 2008, pp. 48–51. Reproduced by permission.

it's a sickness. But still our culture strives to produce and consume more. The question is "why?"

Breakthroughs in brain-scanning science and evolutionary psychology suggest the real culprit is us—or rather the way we play fast and loose with our primitive, instinctive brains. Our basic evolutionary wiring got us down from the trees and across the world, through Ice Ages, plagues, famines and disasters, right into our age of bounty. This unprecedented success was built upon a voracious strategy of "get more of everything, whenever possible."

Now, however, that strategy is set to dump us on the cosmic ash-heap. In the rich world we have gone from millennia of scarcity to unprecedented abundance. Materially, we have everything we need to be content. Except for a stop-button. An "enough" button.

According to evolutionary biologist Robert Trivets, of Rutgers University, New Jersey, US: "We've evolved to be maximizing machines. There isn't necessarily a mechanism in us that says 'relax.'"

Worse, we have created a modern culture that constantly and powerfully prods our acquisitive instincts, stranding us on a carousel of unfulfilable desire, while our planet's natural resources become depleted and its ecology collapses. The only way to change course is to evolve beyond the mindset of "never-enough."

The desire-driven architecture of our lower, primitive brains evolved during the late Pleistocene era, between 130,000 and 200,000 years ago. It was moulded by the behaviour of groups of half-starved hunter-gatherers who turned into farmers, fretfully watching their crops fail. Those who gave up fell by the wayside; the ones who kept going, who colonised the Earth in only 60,000 years, gave us their genes. Our survivors' brains configure us to keep driving onwards—to operate as perpetual dissatisfaction machines. A study in the *Journal of Neuroscience* in 2007 revealed our minds seem built with fewer mechanisms for feeling pleasure than suffering pangs of desire. The Michigan University testers found the sensations of wanting and liking are run by two separate "hedonic hotspots" deep in the brain. The circuit for wanting seems to have around a third more influence on our behaviour than that for liking.

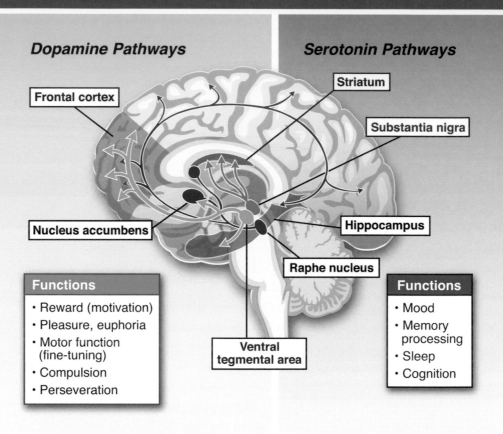

Pleasure-Seeking Centers of the Brain

Dopamine Pathways

- Frontal cortex
- Nucleus accumbens

Functions
- Reward (motivation)
- Pleasure, euphoria
- Motor function (fine-tuning)
- Compulsion
- Perseveration

Ventral tegmental area

Serotonin Pathways

- Striatum
- Substantia nigra
- Hippocampus
- Raphe nucleus

Functions
- Mood
- Memory processing
- Sleep
- Cognition

Taken from: National Institute on Drug Abuse, "Why Do People Abuse Drugs?," *Addiction to Science: From Molecules to Managed Care*. www.drugabuse.gov/pubs/teaching/teaching6/Teaching2.html.

Hard-Wired to Want More

That hard-wiring could wreak considerable environmental impact in itself, but on top of that we evolved as a uniquely acquisitive species, driven to possess things in a way no other creature does. Consider the artefacts found at Neolithic cave sites: hand-axes. Millions of them. Far more than any tool-wielding hominid would have needed. Anthropologists believe that they were not only prized for slicing bison, but also as show-off exemplars of design technology, jagged precursors of Philippe Starck lemon-squeezers. Being able to perform or own fine craftsmanship showed what a high-status, reproductively worthwhile hominid you were.

Nowadays, that instinct has been craftily subverted: we are led to believe we can acquire chunks of mate-pulling mojo by waving credit cards at mass-produced branded items. It's a shame the mojo seems to wear off so fast, but that's what keeps our wasteful system whirring—there's always a more impressive hand-axe substitute ready to come off the production line.

In effect, our acquisitive minds are wired for wasteful buying. Brain scans by scientists at Emory University, in Atlanta, Georgia, show how the neurotransmitter dopamine, one of our brain's powerful reward chemicals, is released in waves as shoppers ponder buying a product. But dopamine is about the hunt, not the trophy; only anticipation stimulates its release. After the deal is sealed, the chemical high flattens in minutes, often leaving a regret known as "buyer's remorse."

But there's always a new next thing to want. Marketing departments have refined an endlessly enticing strategy of constant special offers, latest models and limited editions with added extras. This plants in our famine-sensitive, Stone Age brains the worrying illusion of scarcity, despite the abundance surrounding us. It's the kind of "First World angst" that gets affluent women ripping off each other's limbs in the sales to get this season's must-have frocks.

The Celebrity Effect
Still more enticing to our Stone Age instincts is the fact that all the new products appear to be owned by beautiful people, whether Liz Hurley in ecstasies over some cosmetics or Daniel Craig manfully tapping on a product-placed laptop while pretending to be James Bond. Our minds tend to over-identify with celebrities because we evolved in small tribal groups. If you knew someone they knew you. Our minds still work this way—and give us the idea that the celebs we see so much are our acquaintances.

Humans are also born imitators. This talent underlies much of our species' success—it enabled us to adapt to changing environments far quicker than our competitors could via biological evolution alone, what gets us far ahead of other primates is our attention to detail. A chimp can watch another poking a stick into an ant-hill and mimic the basic idea, but only humans can replicate a technique exactly. We need to choose with great care who we copy, so we have evolved to emulate the habits, idiosyncrasies and clothes of the most successful people we see, hoping imitation will elevate us to their rank. This helps explain why many of us feel compelled to try to keep up materially with celebrities, the mythical alphas in our global village.

There is a dark side to the celeb effect, though. We've grown to despise being out of the in-crowd. Scans by the National Institute of Mental Health, in Maryland, US, show that when we feel socially inferior two brain regions become more active: the insula and the ventral striatum. The former is linked with the gutsinking sensation you get when someone makes you look just "that big," the latter with motivation and reward.

To stave off the pain of feeling second-rate, we get compelled to barricade ourselves behind social acquisitions. That mechanism would have kept our ancestors competitively stretching for the next rung of social evolution ("Oh my gods, darling, look: the Proto-Joneses have entered the Bronze Age"), but in the 21st-century it has locked us into a Pyrrhic battle [a victory that comes with devastating losses]—because the folks next door can also just-about afford all the latest status symbols.

We also mistake designer brands for friends.

Our ancient brain circuits are configured to relate primarily to other people and animals, but this way of relating often gets attached to inanimate objects. We habitually anthropomorphise, which is why so many of us call our cars "she." A report in the *Journal of Advertising Research* in 2000 says we do the same with brands. The branded products we buy are painstakingly created to encourage us to identify with them, to believe they share the same kind of human values we do. We can even believe brands have attitudes towards us, and so develop tight "primary" relationships as we would with friends. In effect, we subconsciously think we are hanging out with impressive tribe-mates.

Buying Purpose

Some of our acquisitiveness can be blamed on a mass spiritual crisis, on trying to buy purpose in a deity-free cosmos. Easter eggs and Christmas pressies [presents] aside, secular life has little use for religious co-branding. Many in the West believe the old omnipotent God is dead and that no-one watches over us. Our only shot at immortality is to achieve acclaim in this material world by piling up stuff. It's a form of existential dummy-sucking. How, indeed, would millions define their sense of purpose if there weren't shopping? This links in to a fascinating theory that shopping isn't just "retail therapy," but a way of buttressing our shaky mental universe. In a 1992 paper entitled "Why Do People Need Self-esteem?," published in the *Journal of Personality and Social Psychology*, American psychologist Thomas Pyszcynski developed the "terror-management theory." Retail-supported self-esteem is, he argues, "a shield designed to control the potential for terror that results from awareness of the horrifying possibility that we humans are merely transient animals groping to survive in a meaningless universe, destined only to die and decay." To mask this possibility, we have created a society that proffers us clothes to transform us into fashion gods, and kitchen utensils to make us domestic deities. Pyszcynski adds that we may have no more significance in the universe than "any individual pineapple or porcupine"—except have you ever seen a porcupine damage the ecosystem with its retail forays?

Shopping Till We Drop?

So here we are, a species that is uniquely wired, compelled, hormonally drugged and scared into wanting things. Perhaps we should resign ourselves to riding the consumptive spiral until we hit eco-geddon. Hell no, argues Aleksandr Solzhenitsyn, the Nobel prize–winning writer and former Soviet dissident. He reckons the only way to revive our sense of human purpose is by not shopping—by reining in our jackdaw urges. Despite his objections to the old Soviet regime, Solzhenitsyn has an equally baleful view of Western consumerist culture. He believes we need to cultivate a sense of unselfish spirituality and politely decline our unprecedented opportunity to use up the planet's resources all at once: "There can be only one true progress: the sum total of the spiritual progresses of individuals. Self-limitation is the fundamental and wisest step of a man who has obtained freedom. It is also the surest path towards its attainment."

That idea might provoke lemon-sucking faces down at the mega-mall, but there seems little alternative environmentally. We have to stop over-revving our never-satisfied primitive instincts and cultivate a society that cools them in favour of more nourishing, non-destructive pathways to satisfaction. We have some evolving to do—and quickly. We need to develop a sense of enough. We must challenge society's overriding message, that we do not yet have all we need to be satisfied. In the West, we have created everything we need as a base for finding contentment. But we're stuck in acquisition mode, rushing past the point beyond which getting more makes life worse rather than better. We have to learn to live "post-more."

This presents difficult challenges. We have never before been environmentally compelled to invent our own constraints—instead we have deep instincts that kick against environmental limits. And our brains find it hard to comprehend the scale and breadth of the problem because they haven't kept pace with the rapid growth of our economic world. Stone Age people had only a few hundred tradeable products—in modern cities there may be 10 billion. The system that produces and sells them appeared in the past 250 years—too sudden for our mental hardware.

Meanwhile, consumerism helpfully tries to blind us to our problems. Modern life is so padded with minor preoccupations about fashion, style, personal growth—the self-obsessed stuff that constantly primps our primitive egotism—that it's hard to recognize the eco-threat as sufficiently monstrous to make our culture do more than gesture at it.

To have any impact, the argument must be framed for our current preoccupations. It must address the personal, rather than anything huge, distant, amorphous or (thanks to our cynicism about politics and media) cornily altruistic. We have to appeal to the overstimulated primitive ego-brain. An answer may lie in not talking about global warming and sustainability, but in personal warming and personal sustainability. Because amid the global warming we are seeing more personal warning: more anxiety and depression; more melting of our circuits; more diseases of excess such as obesity and drug dependency. People complain their lives are too harried and stressed: they are unsustainable. Enoughness is about a personal ecology, about finding our own optimum sustainable balance. It's about saying, "That's enough for me."

Advertising has made us a species that is wired, compelled, and scared into wanting things.

Returning to an Elegant Sufficiency

The idea is an ancient one. It reaches back to an older, wiser, form of self-fulfilment. Before it was marginalised by consumerism, the art of finding one's point of enoughness had been debated by sages since Aristotle. Constant consumption may feel normal and natural, but it is a relatively recent fad. In 18th-century Europe, frugal-cool was a lifestyle choice. Outside royal courts, luxury goods were often spurned, thanks to "worldly asceticism," a Calvinist idea offering the hope of salvation through diligent use of God's gifts (aka planet Earth). Puritans and Quakers promoted the ideal of "Christianity writ plain," where it was considered good to produce and bad to consume more than necessity required. Those living luxuriously were criticised for squandering resources that might support others.

And if we want to make our minds content then brain-scanning science shows there are far more nourishing and sustainable alternatives to spending one's life getting and consuming. Research shows that practicing gratitude for the bounties surrounding us is an effective way of bolstering our morale (though it requires us to reject our "been there, done that, it's soooo yesterday" culture). And although modern media encourage us to fear our neighbours and to compete with each other, brain research increasingly shows that social co-operation, real face-to-face networking and acting generously towards each other can fill our heads with reward chemicals more effectively than the next pair of new shoes ever could.

To turn such things into our mainstream priorities would require a huge evolution in social behaviour. But we can't even stop there: most of all, declaring "enough" demands that we all challenge our own internal propaganda, the messages that get supercharged by our consumerist get-more, be-more culture. Yes, our brains feel immortal. Yes, they whisper that (in the poet Walt Whitman's words) we can contain multitudes. Yes, our minds tell us that we can have it all and do everything. But in fact, no, our brains aren't immortal, and we can't have it all. Those are simply convictions our heads evolved to persuade our bodies out of bed on cold mornings.

We are human and limited, and have to live within our lives' realistic limits. We can hit personal bests, but there will be many things we'll never own, or see, or be or do. Enoughism requires us to accept that the carrot of infinite promise will always dangle just beyond our noses. Embracing this is a path towards contentment and away from eco-geddon. The alternative is for us to wind up as a species that failed to make its next evolutionary step, and condemned itself to remain whining, stressed and angry primitives, greedily grasping for more until the day came when there was simply nothing left to grasp.

TEN

American Consumers Are Becoming More Careful Spenders

Noreen O'Leary

Noreen O'Leary, writing here for *Mediaweek*, a business magazine for the commercial media industry, examines consumer spending habits in the economic downturn, particularly the spending habits of baby boomers. She concludes that this recession is more than an economic downturn; rather it is a seismic shift in the global economy. People are reevaluating their spending decisions and brand loyalties, she reports, looking for value above all. If consumers can spend less to get a latte at McDonald's rather than Starbucks or their favorite television program through the Internet rather than expensive cable, they probably will.

American consumers have no recollection of life in the Great Depression. Not only are most simply too young to remember it, but for the last quarter century they've lived without extended economic hardship, becoming ever more acquisitive in a world of instant gratification and easy credit. No one knows how long or severe the current downturn will be. The circumstances of this recession are unprecedented in the history of modern consumerism: For a generation that has substituted

Noreen O'Leary, "Squeeze Play," *Mediaweek*, January 12, 2009, pp. S8–S9. Copyright © 2009 Nielsen Business Media. All rights reserved. Reproduced by permission of e5 Global Media, LLC.

rising home equity and stock prices for personal savings, the current economic meltdown—with the value of the Dow Jones Industrial Index plunging 40 percent from its peak and $4 trillion lost in home equity—has been psychologically wrenching after a quarter century of unquestioned prosperity.

Factor in the loss of confidence in financial institutions and an investing world where even the very rich can be wiped out through Ponzi schemes [a fraudulent investment or scam] and you have a group of shell-shocked consumers who are reconsidering long-held spending habits.

Much has been made about the everyday stuff of thrifty consumerism—coupon clipping, fewer restaurant meals, brown-bagging it to work, staying close to home for vacations. But those thumbnail sketches of a contracting economy miss the big picture: The fears among baby boomers, who account for more than half of U.S. spending and who traditionally have grown more affluent with age.

Eric Almquist, a Bain & Co. [a global management consulting firm] partner, points to the number of retirement-age individuals who are becoming more conservative with money. "One of the unique things in the Western world now is that you have a huge group of pre-retirement baby boomers, a huge number of people who are asking, 'Can I live off my savings and social security for the rest of my life?'" observes Almquist. "This creates the potential to switch behaviors. They'll watch pennies more closely, be more careful with credit, avoid losses and be more risk adverse, preserve the status quo, rather than gain gains."

Americans Are Saving More

Already there are signs of that change. In one of the most dramatic reversals in post–World War II history, Americans—who in recent years have had negative savings rate—are expected to flip those patterns, with Goldman Sachs now saying the U.S. savings rate could be as high as 6 percent to 10 percent this year.

"This is not a normal recession. This is a tectonic, structural shift, a global realignment," says Umair Haque, director

Americans are becoming more cost conscious as of late. It has even affected the earnings of McDonald's and Starbucks because people think four dollars goes a lot further at McDonald's than it goes at Starbucks.

of Havas Media Lab. "The post-war industrial era was the era of production. Now we're seeing the birth of the real 21st-century economy and marketing has to adapt. We'll see a world where consumption [will] slow—especially in developed countries where there will be a shift from consuming to saving—and production will slow."

Gallup chief economist Dennis Jacobe concurs that "a fundamental change is taking place" in the behavior of U.S. consumers, even if it's not clear how permanent it will be. While gas prices have dropped 57 percent since peaking last July [2008], cheaper petrol has done little to loosen consumer purse strings. And for more affluent American households, their declining confidence and spending track with a time line that started last fall with

Lehman Brothers' bankruptcy filing, and worsened with the once-unimaginable sale and bailouts of troubled financial institutions that quickly followed.

"Last year as gas prices rose, lower-end consumers pulled back and those in the higher end continued to spend, using home equity and credit cards," Jacobe says. "That began to change in mid-September as everything unwound. Even for the rich it's not fashionable to be spending right now."

Frugality in Fashion

As the country's excesses were laid bare with the collapse of its debt culture and layoffs mounted, a new sense of back-to-basics frugality and common sense has taken hold. It's as much an attitudinal backlash as it reflects diminished assets, and it didn't take long for advertising to appropriate the mood in everything from coffee to gems. Last month, for instance, a Seattle McDonald's franchise operator taunted Starbucks in its hometown with billboards proclaiming: "Large is the new grande" and "Four bucks is dumb." In its fourth-quarter pitch, De Beers positioned diamonds as something to be passed down among generations in a world of "disposable distractions." Whether bling-seeking consumers buy into copy like "here's to less," the sentiments seem to sum up the larger mood of the country.

"The last cataclysmic event was 9/11, caused by a terrorist attack. It was patriotic to get out and shop," says Alison Burns, global client services director, JWT, New York. "This downfall is of our *own* making—greed, mismanagement and all sorts of things much closer to home. Now it's not patriotic to go shopping. It's all about being prudent, back to basics, valuing the things we have more highly."

Allstate Insurance addresses the economy head-on in new work with spokesman Dennis Haysbert standing in front of Depression-era photos while talking about how in tough times "people start enjoying the small things in life: a home-cooked meal, time with loved ones, appreciating the things we do have."

"There's rapid change under way. Consumers seem to be right-sizing and looking for smart money management," says Lisa Cochrane, Allstate's vp, marketing.

Ben Kline, CMO [chief marketing officer] at Allstate agency Leo Burnett U.S.A., says that for consumers it's not just a matter of cutting back, it's about their reassessing what's important.

The Death of "Perceived Value"

"We're seeing a shift from a trade-up culture to a trade-*off* culture," he explains. "'What brands are going to be part of my life, which ones are indispensable or dispensable?' Value alone is not a differentiator; there will be value or there won't be a sale. Marketers will do well in understanding how to frame the trade off and reintroduce themselves."

American Spending Habits Have Changed Permanently

Percentage of Americans Who Are Spending Less than They Used to, and Whether This Is a New Normal or Temporary

	April 2009	July 2009	February 2010
Spending Less Money as a New Normal Pattern	32%	32%	38%
Spending Less Money as a Temporary Change	21%	18%	19%

Taken from: Dennis Jacobe, "Spending Less Becoming Norm for Many Americans," *Gallup*, February 25, 2010. www.gallup.com/poll/126197/Spending-Less-Becoming-New-Norm-Americans.aspx.

Kline, whose agency works for McDonald's, adds: "The 'apex predators' of categories that didn't add enough value as consumers traded up are going to be in trouble. People are realizing they don't need a $4 latte; $4 goes further at McDonald's."

Which may go some way in explaining the disparate results of the two iconic brands: In the fiscal fourth quarter, ended Sept. 28 [2008], Starbucks reported a 96 percent drop in quarterly earnings growth while McDonald's reported an 11 percent increase in its Sept. 30th third quarter. The definition of value may have less to do with increased unit sales and more with actual consumer benefits.

"In the industrial era, we were good at creating perceived value. But now people are getting back to basics and the future of marketing is to create real value," says Haque of Havas' Media Lab. "Perceived value is for consumers; real value is for people. Perceived value is about how much can we get people to consume and that is patently at odds with the new realities of the economy. Real value delivers long-term outcomes, making people smarter, better off, healthier."

A Shift in Media Consumption

Even with America's No. 1 pastime, media, consumers are reevaluating their spending. Last summer, as gas prices peaked, Mediaedge:cia asked consumers in smaller, rural counties what their priorities were. Food came in at the top, followed by gas to get to work, cell phones and broadband. Interestingly, TV was not among those top choices.

"We've reached a plateau about whether people are really getting their money's worth," underscores Lee Doyle, North American CEO, Mediaedge:cia, who says the average U.S. household spends $270 a month on communication technology services. "This is going to accelerate what is already starting to happen: People are going to discover things like Hulu [a free, online streaming video, TV and movie provider] that much faster because they're strapped. It's not just techies, it's the Wal-Mart consumer. Whether it's Netflix or DVDs from the library or the wealth of video online, that's scary for marketers. It just accelerates what we know about consumers as being more and more in control of their media."

There is, of course, the irony that as consumers do the right thing for themselves by saving more, they hurt the economy's chances of revival by spending less, the "paradox of thrift" as put forth by [economist] John Maynard Keynes. To be sure, younger U.S. consumers haven't suffered the financial reversals of their elders. Their spending may be temporarily reined in during the current credit crunch, but they have a love of brands and their acquisitive tastes show little signs of giving up instant gratification and a "luxuries-as-necessities" lifestyle.

A New Consumer Mind-Set

But back in the larger world, there are macro challenges, beyond boomers' fears about funding retirement, which could further thwart a return to healthy spending.

Robert J. Samuelson, author of the new book, *The Great Inflation and Its Aftermath: The Past and Future of Affluence*, says the coming era may usher in a new consumer mind-set he describes as "affluent deprivation." People will feel poorer because at the same time their income growth slows, they'll be paying more towards higher taxes, energy costs and healthcare. "When people think of their standard of living, they think of discretionary spending, which has always been an expression of their freedom," says Samuelson, a *Newsweek* writer. "While their income may not go down, their discretionary spending could remain stagnant or decline."

The global financial crisis has, of course, slowed growth in previously hot, emerging economies like China. Less obvious may be the population drop in large Western European markets. Bain & Co.'s Almquist notes that there is a declining populace in countries like Spain, Portugal, Italy and Germany. "Marketers face not only the possible change toward more conservative boomer behavior, pre-retirement, they're also going to have fewer customers there in absolute numbers. Marketers are going to have to be relentlessly focused on where value is and on their core customers. It's not going to be like the 1950s where you can throw anything out there and see growth," he says.

What You Should Know About Consumer Culture

In the United States, Teens Are Powerful Consumers

According to the May 2006 *Congressional Quarterly Researcher*:

- Teens in the United States spent $159 billion of their own money in 2005.
- About 10 percent of teens have credit cards, and nearly twice that have debit cards.
- Most teens spend their money on food, movies, and personal items; less than a third help with family finances or save their money.

Globally, Teens Are Powerful Consumers

According to the *TRU Study: 2009 Global Teen Edition*, teens are a quickly growing segment of the world population with significant spending power.

- Twelve- to 19-year-olds make up nearly 461 million of the world's population with $592 billion in purchasing power.
- In developed markets, 17 million 12- to 19-year-olds have $268 billion in purchasing power.
- In emerging markets 41 million 12- to 19-year-olds have $324 billion in purchasing power.
- In the United States, 33.9 million 12- to 19-year-olds have $176 billion in purchasing power.
- By contrast, in India, 181.9 million 12- to 19-year-olds have $45 billion in purchasing power.

Globally, Consumer Spending Is Unequal

According to the World Bank Development Indicators (2008):

- The world's richest 20 percent consume 76.6 percent of the world's goods.
- The world's middle 60 percent consume 21.19 percent of the world's goods.
- The world's poorest 20 percent consume 1.5 percent of the world's goods.

According to the United Nations Development Programme, the richest fifth of the world's population

- consume 45 percent of all fish and meat while the poorest fifth consume 5 percent,
- consume 58 percent of all global energy while the poorest fifth consume less than 4 percent,
- consume 84 percent of all paper while the poorest fifth consume 1.1 percent,
- own 87 percent of all the world's vehicles while the poorest fifth own less than 1 percent.

Most American Teens Believe That "Things" Will Make Them Happy

According to Shira Boss, a journalist and the author of *Green with Envy*:

- More than 56 percent of young adults between the ages of fourteen and twenty say that "having a rich lifestyle" is a top priority for them, according to a study by the PNC Financial Group;
- Almost three-quarters of teens said they would be happier if they had more money to spend on themselves, according to a survey by Harris Interactive.

Teens Are Spending Less, but Not on Everything

According to *Advertising Age* magazine, during this recession teens have adjusted their spending.

- Teen joblessness reached 22 percent in March 2009, the highest in a decade.

- Overall, teens were spending about 14 percent less during the spring of 2009 than they were the year before.
- In particular, teens are spending less on clothing, beauty products, movies, concerts, and sporting events.
- Teens seem to be cutting back the most on restaurant spending, which decreased 20 percent from the fall of 2007 to the fall of 2009.
- During the same period, teens actually slightly increased their spending on personal home entertainment such as DVDs, music, and video games.

Debt Affects Many Teens and Young Adults

The Washington State Department of Financial Institutions has compiled the following statistics regarding money and young people in the United States:

- One small study of 18- and 19-year-olds found that 21 percent have credit cards.
- On average 18- to 24-year-olds spend almost 30 percent of their income repaying debts. That is double the percentage that age group spent on debt in 1992 and triple the recommended amount.
- The bankruptcy rate among 18- to 24-year-olds has nearly doubled.
- In 2002 more people filed for bankruptcy than graduated from college.
- More students drop out of college due to financial problems than due to academic problems, according to university administrators.
- Forty-five percent of all college students are in credit card debt.

According to a 2008 article in the *Collector*, a publication from the American Collector's Association International:

- Nearly one-quarter of students leave college with more than $5,000 in credit card debt.
- One in ten students leaves college with more than $10,000 in credit card debt.
- The average student leaves college with $2,748 in credit card debt; paying only the minimum payments at an interest rate of 15 percent, that debt, plus $2,506.01 in interest, would take almost eighteen years to repay.

What You Should Do About Consumer Culture

Sixty-eight percent of all children in the United States ages eight to eighteen have televisions in their bedrooms. The typical American seventh grader spends three hours a day watching television. On average, American children and teens watch between twenty-five thousand and forty thousand commercials every year. Every year $15 billion to $17 billion are spent advertising to children in the United States. U.S. teens alone spend about $160 billion every year. The pervasive consumer culture in America definitely concerns its teens. What can teens do?

First, make yourself conscious of advertising. Whether online, on television, on billboards, or even at school, watch for media messages and activate your inner critic. According to the Better Business Bureau, here are some questions to get you started:

- What is the first thing that you notice in the advertisement?
- What in the ad is attractive or unattractive?
- What is the ad actually advertising?
- How does the ad make you feel about what is advertised?
- What questions should you ask yourself before buying or buying into what is advertised?

Also ask yourself how the ad makes you feel about yourself. Remember that ads often work by making you feel insecure about yourself and subtly (or sometimes not so subtly) suggesting that whatever is being advertised will make everything better. If you notice an ad that you think is dishonest or unfair, you can voice your opinion by contacting the network directly or by complaining to the Federal Communications Commission. A more personal and more immediate action, however, might be to discuss the ads and their messages with your friends and family.

You can also resist the consumer culture by making yourself a conscious consumer. When you are shopping—in a store or online—ask yourself why. Are you attempting to cheer yourself up, to create confidence, to express yourself, to keep up with your friends, or are you buying something that you really need? If you are not sure, postpone your purchase and think about it. If you decide that you are just trying to make yourself feel better or create your identity, look for another way to do it. Instead of buying new, expensive sports equipment, practice your sport more often; instead of buying a new trendy outfit, handbag, or prom dress, remake something you have or trade items with friends; instead of cheering yourself up with more "stuff," sort through what you have, appreciate what you love, and donate the rest to a charity resale shop. If you are shopping for something that you really do need, ask yourself if you could be more practical. Could you rewire, repaint, or update that lamp that is a problem or outdated instead of heading to that superstore? Could you pay to have that zipper fixed in your favorite pair of jeans instead of going to the mall? Could you find those dorm room accessories at a resale shop, yard sale, or in your parent's basement instead of buying everything new? Could you find that book, DVD, CD, or video game at your local library or borrow it from a friend instead of buying it?

Get practical about other expenditures as well. Plan a movie night in with your friends instead of a movie night out. Instead of ordering pizza delivery, get creative and make your own. Instead of getting your hair and nails done at a salon for prom, do your own, or get a couple of friends together and do each others' hair and nails. Instead of buying your parents expensive birthday presents, detail their cars, make them a nice dinner, or surprise them by cleaning out the garage.

Another important way that teens can help is to educate themselves about and take charge of their own finances. If your school offers a course that covers personal finances, take it. If the school does not offer it, make a case for one and present it to your school administrators. Get involved with clubs and organizations at school or outside of school where you can learn about money. Most clubs and student councils have a budget and fund-raisers, where you can gain personal experience. If you can, talk to older family members about their financial experiences—both positive and negative. Ask your parents to show you how they budget their finances and balance their checkbook, if they do. You can also consult the "Organizations to Contact" at the end of this book for publications and tutorials. Next, apply what you learn and take charge of your own finances. Save your receipts and track your spending for a week or a month and then set personal goals—for both spending and saving.

Finally, you may look for meaning outside of "stuff." Get to know yourself and what you feel passionate about—besides your things. Learn more about the world and its people, and think of yourself as a world citizen. How can you use your skills and interests to make a real difference in the world? Your next-door neighbors, the next town or state, or halfway around the world—whatever most interests you—does not matter as long as you venture outside of yourself and your own "world" and contribute instead of consume.

ORGANIZATIONS TO CONTACT

The editors have compiled the following list of organizations concerned with the issues debated in this book. The descriptions are derived from materials provided by the organizations. All have publications or information available for interested readers. The list was compiled on the date of publication of the present volume; the information provided here may change. Be aware that many organizations take several weeks or longer to respond to inquiries, so allow as much time as possible for the receipt of requested materials.

Cato Institute
1000 Massachusetts Ave. NW, Washington, DC 20001-5403
(202) 842-0200
website: www.cato.org

Founded in 1977, the mission of the Cato Institute is to increase the understanding of public policies based on the principles of limited government, free markets, individual liberty, and peace. The institute aims to use the most effective means to originate, advocate, promote, and disseminate applicable policy proposals that create free, open, and civil societies in the United States and throughout the world.

Consumer Action
221 Main St., Ste. 480, San Francisco, CA 94105
(415) 777-9635
website: www.consumer-action.org

Consumer Action is a nonprofit, membership-based organization that was founded in San Francisco in 1971. Consumer Action has continued to serve consumers nationwide by advancing consumer rights; referring consumers to complaint-handling agencies through its free hotline; publishing materials in Chinese, English, Korean, Spanish, Vietnamese, and other languages; advocating for consumers in the media and before lawmakers; and comparing prices on credit cards, bank accounts, and long-distance services.

Consumer Federation of America (CFA)
1620 I St. NW, Ste. 200, Washington, DC 20006
(202) 387-6121
e-mail: cfa@consumerfed.org
website: http://consumerfed.org

The CFA gathers facts, analyzes issues, and disseminates information to the public, policy makers, and the rest of the consumer movement. The size and diversity of its membership—approximately 280 nonprofit organizations throughout the nation with a combined membership exceeding 50 million people—enables CFA to speak for virtually all consumers. In particular, CFA advocates for those who have the greatest needs, especially the least affluent.

Consumer Watchdog
1750 Ocean Park Blvd., Ste. 200, Santa Monica, CA 90405
(310) 392-0522
e-mail: admin@consumerwatchdog.org
website: www.consumerwatchdog.org

Consumer Watchdog (formerly the Foundation for Taxpayer and Consumer Rights) is a nationally recognized consumer group that has been fighting corrupt corporations and dishonest politicians since 1985. Over the years, Consumer Watchdog has worked to save Americans billions of dollars and improved countless peoples' lives by speaking out on behalf of patients, ratepayers, and policyholders.

Credit Abuse Resistance Education Program (CARE)
Andrea M. Siderakis, Judicial Assistant to Hon. John C. Ninfo, II
U.S. Bankruptcy Court, 1400 U.S. Courthouse
100 State Street, Rochester, NY 14614
(585) 613-4290
e-mail: careprogram@nywb.uscourts.gov
website: www.careprogram.us

CARE is a free financial literacy program that makes bankruptcy professionals throughout the United States available to educators, students, and the public to illuminate the dangers of credit abuse. Articles written specifically for teens are available through its website as well as materials for high school teachers and an online credit education program called FoolProof "Solo" that teens can complete on their own.

Federal Trade Commission (FTC)
Consumer Response Center, Washington, DC 20580
(877) 382-4357
website: www.ftc.gov

The FTC deals with issues that touch the economic life of every American. It is the only federal agency with consumer protection and competition jurisdiction in broad sectors of the economy. The FTC pursues vigorous and effective law enforcement; advances consumers' interests by sharing its expertise with federal and state legislatures and U.S. and international government agencies; develops policy and research tools through hearings, workshops, and conferences; and creates practical and plain-language educational programs for consumers and businesses in a global marketplace with constantly changing technologies.

Free Market Foundation (FMF)
903 East Eighteenth St., Ste. 230, Plano, TX 75074
(972) 423-8889
fax: (972) 423-8899
e-mail: info@freemarket.org
website: www.freemarket.org

The FMF, which was founded in 1972, is a nonprofit organization dedicated to protecting freedoms and strengthening families in Texas and nationwide. It stands for First Amendment freedoms, less government, and solid family values. FMF is one of the few groups in the country that has a legislative and legal department, Liberty Legal Institute, staffed with full-time attorneys experienced in litigation.

Green America
1612 K St. NW, Ste. 600, Washington, DC 20006
(800) 584-7336
website: www.coopamerica.org

Green America is a not-for-profit membership organization founded in 1982, going by the name Co-op America until January 1, 2009. Its mission is to harness economic power—the strength of consumers, investors, businesses, and the marketplace—to create a socially just and environmentally sustainable society.

National Consumers League (NCL)
1701 K St. NW, Ste. 1200, Washington, DC 20006
(202) 835-3323
e-mail: info@nclnet.org
website: www.nclnet.org

The NCL has represented consumers and workers on marketplace and workplace issues since its founding in 1899. The NCL provides government, businesses, and other organizations with the consumer's perspective on concerns including child labor, privacy, food safety, and medication information. The NCL is home to the Child Labor Coalition; NCL's Fraud Center; SOS Rx Coalition; and the LifeSmarts program, a quiz-show style competition designed to develop the consumer and marketplace knowledge and skills of teenagers.

SustainAbililty
Washington Office, 1638 R St. NW,
Ste. 301, Washington, DC 20009
(202) 315-4150
e-mail: washington@sustainability.com
website: www.sustainability.com

Established in 1987, SustainAbility advises clients on the risks and opportunities associated with corporate responsibility and sustainable development. Working at the interface between market forces and societal expectations, it seeks solutions to social and environmental challenges that deliver long-term value.

SustainAbility's research addresses topics as diverse as the future of globalization, lobbying, governance, supply chains, and corporate accountability.

Truth About Credit
44 Winter St., Boston, MA 02108
(617) 747-4330
website: http://truthaboutcredit.org

Truth About Credit is a project of the U.S. Public Interest Research Group (PIRG) Education Fund and the Student PIRGs. U.S. PIRG works to pursue a mission of standing up to powerful interests on behalf of the public. U.S. PIRG conducts research, education, and advocacy on behalf of consumers. With the help of a professional staff of advocates and organizers, the Student PIRGs investigate problems and develop practical solutions and aim to convince the media and decision makers to pay attention and take action on consumer protection and higher education issues.

BIBLIOGRAPHY

Books

Benjamin R. Barber, *Consumed: How Markets Corrupt Children, Infantilize Adults, and Swallow Citizens Whole*. New York: Norton, 2007.

Jessica Blatt, *The Teen Girl's Gotta-Have-It Guide to Money: Getting Smart About Making It, Saving It, and Spending It!* New York: Watson-Guptill, 2008.

Howard Bloom, *The Genius of the Beast: A Radical Re-vision of Capitalism*. Amherst, NY: Prometheus, 2009.

Shira Boss, *Green with Envy: Why Keeping Up with the Joneses Is Keeping Us in Debt*. New York: Grand Central, 2006.

Christopher Greenslate and Kerri Leonard, *On a Dollar a Day: One Couple's Unlikely Adventures in Eating in America*. New York: Hyperion, 2010.

Shannon Hayes, *Radical Homemakers: Reclaiming Domesticity from a Consumer Culture*. Richmondville, NY: Left to Write, 2010.

Annie Leonard, *The Story of Stuff: How Our Problem with Overconsumption Is Trashing the Planet, Our Communities and Our Health—and What to Do About It*. New York: Free Press, 2010.

Carrie McLaren and Jason Torchinsky, eds., *Ad Nauseam: A Survivor's Guide to American Consumer Culture*. New York: Farrar, 2009.

Kevin Salwen and Hannah Salwen, *The Power of Half: One Family's Decision to Stop Talking and Start Giving Back*. Boston: Houghton Mifflin Harcourt, 2010.

Ellen Ruppel Shell, *Cheap: The High Cost of Discount Culture*. New York: Penguin, 2009.

Susan Gregory Thomas, *Buy, Buy Baby: How Consumer Culture Manipulates Parents and Harms Young Minds*. Boston: Mariner, 2009.

Rob Walker, *Buying In: The Secret Dialogue Between What We Buy and Who We Are*. New York: Random House, 2008.

Periodicals and Internet Sources

Daniel Akst, "Buyer's Remorse," *Wilson Quarterly*, Winter 2004.

Mark Anielski, "Are We Happy Yet? All the Money in the World Won't Buy It, So What Are We Working For?," *Alternatives Journal*, 2009.

Farah Banihali, "Consumerism: It's Barbie's World," *Altmuslimah*, July 29, 2009. www.altmuslimah.com/a/b/a/3213.

Rachel Barnes, "Ethical Shopping: Is It a Meaningless Concept?," *Grocer*, February 9, 2008.

Ryan Beiler, "The Tao of Dumpster Diving. Why Scavenge? You Get a Lot of Really Good Food That's Really, Really Free," *Sojourners*, May 2006.

Matt Carmichael, "Radical Rest: In Addressing Tiredness We Address the Problem of Unsustainability," *Resurgence*, May/June, 2008.

CQ Researcher, "Teen Spending," May 26, 2006.

Charlotte Downes, "Anti Consumerism: A Freegan Story," *Taste the Waste*, October 19, 2009. www.tastethewaste.com/article/20091019-Anti-Consumerism-A-Freegan-Story.

Economist, "The End of the Affair; Spending and the Economy," November 22, 2008.

Ferne Edwards and David Mercer, "Gleaning from Gluttony: An Australian Youth Subculture Confronts the Ethics of Waste," *Australian Geographer*, November 2007.

Barbara Ehrenreich, "Fall of the American Consumer," *Nation*, March 11, 2008.

Joseph Epstein, "Lapse of Luxury: True Luxury Has Many Pretenders, Which Is Why It Is in Such Scant Supply," *Town and Country*, January 2008.

GiveMe20.com, "Savvy Stuff: Top Ten Budgeting Basics for Teens." www.moneyandstuff.info/budgetingbasics.html.

Wendee Holtcamp, "My 30 Days of Consumer Celibacy: For a Whole Month, One Writer Practiced a Kind of Abstinence So She Could Better Understand Her Own Complicity in Our Throwaway Culture. It Wasn't Easy," *OnEarth*, Summer 2007.

Courtney Hutchison, "Today's Teens More Anxious, Depressed and Paranoid than Ever: Consumer Culture May Be to Blame, Researchers Say," *ABC News*, December 10, 2009. http://abcnews.go.com/Health/MindMoodNews/todays-teens-anxious-depressed-aranoid/story?id=9281013.

Steve Kendall, "How Looking Poor Became the New Status Symbol," *Details*, June/July 2009.

Richard North, "Consumerism Is Virtuous," *Times* (London), December 29, 2005.

Amy Novotney, "What's Behind American Consumerism?," *Monitor on Psychology*, July/August 2008.

NPR, "Author: Level of Consumerism Is Out of Control," *Morning Edition*. www.npr.org/templates/story/story.php?storyId=102900902.

PsyBlog, "Six Psychological Reasons Consumer Culture Is Unsatisfying," April 2010.www.spring.org.uk/2010/04/six-psychological-reasons-consumer-culture-is-unsatisfying.php.

Charles Shaw, "Viewing Consumer Culture Through the Lens of Addiction," *Huffington Post*, June 6, 2008. www.huffingtonpost.com/charles-shaw/viewing-consumer-culture_b_105750.html.

Anthony Stevens-Arroyo, "Only Bad Capitalists Go to Heaven," *Washington Post*, September 19, 2008.

James Surowiecki, "Inconspicuous Consumption," *New Yorker*, October 12, 2009.

Will Weissert, "Consumerism Good for Cuba's Communism?," *Seattle Times*, April 3, 2008. http://seattletimes.nwsource.com/html/nationworld/2004324033_cuba03.html.

Thad Williamson, "America Beyond Consumerism: Has Capitalist Economic Growth Outlived Its Purpose?," *Dollars & Sense*, May/June 2007.

Jess Worth, "Buy Now, Pay Later," *Utne*, March/April 2007.

INDEX

PICTURE CREDITS